# AESTHETIC FUNCTION, NORM AND VALUE

## AS SOCIAL FACTS

MICHIGAN SLAVIC CONTRIBUTIONS

*a Series Established to Serve
Graduate Slavic Studies*

Department of Slavic
Languages and Literature
The University of Michigan

AESTHETIC FUNCTION, NORM AND VALUE

AS SOCIAL FACTS

Translated from Czech, with notes and afterword
by Mark E. Suino

JAN MUKAŘOVSKÝ

Ann Arbor, 1979

Printed in Ann Arbor, Michigan

# PREFACE

Students and scholars concerned with problems of Slavic literary theory and aesthetics have long been aware of the important position occupied by Jan Mukařovský in these areas. Many of them, however, have not been armed with a reading knowledge of Czech, and thus have been unable to consult his works in their original form (there are formidable obstacles even for those who read Czech with facility). Slavists, then, for whom the works of Mukařovský have been difficult to read (or obtain), constitute a part of the public which this volume hopes to serve.

A different group, one which I suspect is numerically much larger but less homogeneous, also has an interest in translations of the major Czech contributions to the Prague School. This latter group consists of the thousands of American college and university students who have been exposed to *Theory of Literature*, or "Wellek and Warren" as it is usually called.[1] Many readers of *Theory of Literature* have been tantalized by the frequent references to Mukařovský and other members of the Prague School, and then frustrated by the fact that most of their works have not been available in English. The situation is currently being alleviated to some extent in this country. The present volume is intended as a contribution in this direction. It is further

[1] René Wellek and Austin Warren: *Theory of Literature,* N.Y., 1956. While he was in Ann Arbor last year Professor Wellek noted that a number of people seem, indeed, to believe that "Wellek and Warren" is the correct title.

intended as a kind of companion piece to René Wellek's *The Literary Theory and Aesthetics of the Prague School*,[2] in which he has chosen the works of Mukařovský to illustrate the literary activities of the Prague School. In the same study Professor Wellek has provided a bibliography of French, German and English translations of Mukařovský's works.[3]

M.E.S.

---

[2] *Michigan Slavic Contributions*, Ann Arbor, 1969.

[3] Additional remarks on Mukařovský and the Prague School may be found in Victor Erlich: *Russian Formalism*, The Hague, 1965, and in René Wellek: *Concepts of Criticism*, New Haven, 1963. The linguistic activity of the School is outlined in J. Vachek (ed.): *A Prague School Reader in Linguistics*, Bloomington, Indiana, 1964. Cf. also P. Garvin: *A Prague School Reader on Esthetics, Literary Structure and Style*, Washington, D.C., 1964 for selected translations from Mukařovský and the other members of the Prague School.

I

The aesthetic function occupies an important position in the life of individuals and of society as a whole. The number of people who come into direct contact with art is, however, quite restricted, both by the comparative rarity of aesthetic talent—which is sometimes focused on particular areas in art—and by the obstacles of social stratification. For certain strata of society the accessibility of works of art and aesthetic training are limited. Nevertheless some effects of art reach even those people who have no direct contact with it (cf., for example, the influence of poetry on the development of a language system). Moreover, the aesthetic function embraces a much wider area of activity than does art by itself. Any object and any activity, whether natural or human, may become a carrier of the aesthetic function. This statement does not imply panaestheticism, since: 1. it expresses only the possibility but not the necessity of the aesthetic function; 2. it does not claim that the aesthetic function always dominates all other functions of a given phenomenon in the entire area of aesthetics; 3. it neither mixes the aesthetic function with other functions, nor considers other functions as mere variants of the aesthetic function. We only mention it in order to clarify the fact that there is no definite borderline between the aesthetic and the extra-aesthetic. There are no objects or actions which, by virtue of their essence or organization would, regardless of time, place or the person evaluating them, possess an aesthetic function and others which, again by their very nature, would be necessarily

1

immune to the aesthetic function. At first glance this statement might seem to be excessive. One could counter it either with examples of objects and actions which *seem* to be totally incapable of any aesthetic function (e.g., some basic physical activity such as breathing, or very abstract thought processes) or, conversely, with examples of phenomena (namely, works of art) whose entire construction predetermines that they will have an aesthetic effect. Modern art, beginning with Naturalism, does not ignore any area of reality when choosing its subject matter and, beginning with Cubism and similar movements in other branches of art, no restriction is placed on the choice of materials or techniques. Similarly, modern aesthetics places much emphasis on broad aesthetic areas (J. M. Guyau, M. Dessoir and his school, and others). All of the foregoing provides sufficient evidence that even those items which, in the traditional aesthetic view, would not have been credited with any aesthetic potential, can now become aesthetic facts. Note, for example, a statement by Guyau: "To breathe deeply and feel one's blood being cleansed by its contact with the air—is this not precisely an intoxicating experience, and would it not be difficult to deny it an aesthetic value?"[1] Dessoir, too, comments: "If we call a machine, a solution to a mathematical problem or the organization of some social group a beautiful thing, it is more than just a form of expression" (*Aesthetik und allgemeine Kunstwissenschaft,* Stuttgart, 1906). One may also introduce contrary examples in which those same works of art that are the privileged bearers of the aesthetic function can lose it and either be destroyed as superfluous (cf. the obliteration of old frescoes by painting or

[1]*Les problèmes de l'esthétique contemporaine,* Paris, 1913, pp. 20-21.

plastering), or will be used with no consideration for their aesthetic purpose (cf. the transformation of old palaces into barracks, etc.). There are, however—within art and outside of it—objects which, by virtue of their organization are meant to have an aesthetic effect. This is actually the essential property of art. But an active capacity for the aesthetic function is not a real property of an object, even if the object has been deliberately composed with the aesthetic function in mind. Rather, the aesthetic function manifests itself only under certain conditions, i.e. in a certain social context. A phenomenon which, in one time period, country, etc., was the privileged bearer of the aesthetic function may be incapable of bearing this function in a different time, country, etc. In the history of art there is no lack of cases in which the original aesthetic or artistic effect of a certain product was re-discovered only through scientific research.[2]

The limits of the province of aesthetics, therefore, are not provided by reality itself, and are exceedingly changeable. This is particularly evident when we consider the viewpoint of the individual. We have all encountered people for whom anything can acquire an aesthetic function and, conversely, people for whom the aesthetic function exists only to a minimal degree. Even from our own personal experience we know that the borderline between the aesthetic and the extra-aesthetic, depending as it does on the degree of aesthetic perception, fluctuates for each person according to his age, changes in health, and even momentary moods. But as

---

[2]N. S. Trubeckoj: " 'Xoženie Afanasija Nikitina' kak literaturnyj pamjatnik," Versty, I, Paris, 1926, or R. Jagodic: "Der Stil der altrussischen Vitae," Contributions to the Second International Congress of Slavists, Warsaw, 1934.

soon as we consider a social context rather than individual viewpoints, it turns out that despite all transitory individual variations there is a fairly stable distribution of
the aesthetic function in the world of objects and events.
Even then, however, the dividing line between the
domain of the aesthetic function and that of extra-
aesthetic phenomena will not be entirely clear, since
there are many gradations of the aesthetic function and
it is rarely possible to determine the complete absence
of even the weakest aesthetic residue. But it is possible
to ascertain objectively—from certain symptoms—the
presence of the aesthetic function in, e.g., matters of
housing, dress, etc.

       As soon as we change our perspective in time,
space, or even from one social grouping to another (e.g.
from one stratum to another, one generation to
another, etc.) we find a change in the distribution of the
aesthetic function and of its boundaries. The aesthetic
function of food, for instance, is obviously greater in
France than in Czechoslovakia. In our cities the aesthetic
function of clothing is greater among women than among
men, but this difference frequently does not obtain in
rural areas where folk dress is worn. The aesthetic function of clothing also varies according to typical situations involving a particular social context. Thus the
aesthetic function of work clothes is quite weak compared to that of formal attire. In regard to temporal differences it can be shown that, unlike the present-day
custom, as late as the seventeenth century (in the age of
Rococo) the aesthetic function of men's clothing was
just as strong as that of women's clothing. In the period
since the World War the aesthetic function of dress and
building construction has acquired much broader social
dimensions and involves many more situations than before the war.

In separating the aesthetic from the extra-aesthetic, therefore, we must always bear in mind that we are not dealing with precisely defined and mutually exclusive areas. Both are in constant, mutual contact which can be described as a dialectical antinomy. It is not possible to investigate the status or the evolution of the aesthetic function without asking how broadly (or narrowly) it is distributed over the dimensions of reality. We must ask whether its boundaries are relatively well-defined or somewhat vague, whether it occurs evenly over the entire area of society or mainly in a few strata and contexts. And all of the above questions must involve a particular time period and social entity. In other words, in order to characterize the state and development of the aesthetic function it is not enough simply to state where and how it appears, nor to establish to what degree and in which circumstances it is absent or at least weakened.

Let us now turn to the inner organization of the aesthetic area itself. We have already indicated that it is extremely varied, both with respect to the intensity of the aesthetic function in various phenomena and to the distribution of the function among the formations of any given social entity. There is, however, a certain limit which divides the entire, heterogeneous aesthetic area into two basic parts, depending on the relative importance of the aesthetic function as compared to other functions. This is the line which separates art from extra-artistic aesthetic phenomena. The boundary between art and all other aesthetic areas, and even extra-aesthetic areas, is important not only for aesthetics, but also for the history of art, since the definition of this boundary is crucial to the choice of historical material. It would appear that a work of art is clearly defined by a certain texture (manner of execution). But actually this criterion holds, and not without some qualification, only for the social context to which the work is (or was) originally addressed.[3] When we confront a product whose origin is connected with a society which is temporally or spatially distant from us, we can not judge it according to our own system of values. We have already noted that it is frequently necessary to determine, through a complex scientific procedure, whether such a product, in its original social context, was a work of art. We can never discount the possibility that the functions of a given work were originally entirely different from what they appear to be when we apply our system of values. In addition, the transition from art to what lies outside is always gradual and often nearly indiscernible. Let us take architecture as an example: building construction as a whole presents us with a continuous series, from products with no aesthetic function all the way to works of art, and often it is impossible to ascertain that point in the series where art begins. Actually it is never possible to determine it exactly, even if we are considering buildings within our own social context. The difficulty is naturally greater when we are dealing with products which, due to their remoteness in space or time, appear exotic to us. Finally, there is a third difficulty which E. Utitz noted *"Kunstsein ist etwas ganz anderes als Kunstwert."*[4] In other words: the question of the aesthetic evaluation of art works is fundamentally different from the question of the limits of art. Even an art work which in our view is bad belongs within the realms of art, for that is why we evaluate it as we do. In practice it is very difficult to comply with this theoretical

---

[3]Cf. the case of the statute *L'age d'or* by Rodin. It was originally criticized for being merely a cast of an actual human body.

[4]*Grundlegung der allgemeinen Kunstwissenschaft*, II, Stuttgart, 1920, p. 5.

principle, particularly in respect to so-called peripheral art or such objects as, in the words of J. Čapek, "most modest art." If we should inquire about such products (e.g. "novels for servants" or illustrations used in advertising) whether they function as art, it can easily happen that we would confuse identification of function with evaluation.

Obviously the transitions between art, on the one hand, and the extra-artistic and extra-aesthetic on the other, are so imperceptible, and it is so difficult to isolate them, that it is illusory to imagine that we can formulate precise boundaries between them. Must we then abandon all attempts to discover the boundaries? In spite of everything we feel too strongly that the division between art and the areas of merely "aesthetic" phenomena is a fundamental one. Wherein does this division lie? In the fact that in art the aesthetic function is the dominant function, while outside of art, even if it is present, it occupies a secondary position. As a refutation of this position one might object that in art, too, it often happens that the aesthetic function either on the part of the author or of the public is programmatically subordinated to another function. Note, for example, the demand for tendentiousness in art. But this objection is not convincing: as long as a work is spontaneously assigned to the realm of art, any emphasis on a function other than the aesthetic function is treated as a polemic against the essential aims of art and not as a normal case. The predominance of some extra-aesthetic function is a rather frequent phenomenon in the history of art; but the dominance of the aesthetic function in such cases is always felt as fundamental, "unmarked," while dominance by another function is considered "marked," i.e. as a violation of the normal condition. This relationship between the aesthetic function and other functions of art follows *logically* from the nature of art as the province of phenomena which are *per se* aesthetic.[5] Finally, let us recall that the assumption of the dominance of the aesthetic function has total validity only when mutual differentiation of functions exists. There are, however, environments in which there is no systematic differentiation of functions, e.g., society in the Middle Ages or in folklore, and even in such cases, although a mutual subordination and domination of functions can be shifted through evolution, it can not proceed to the point where one of them would completely and clearly dominate the others in a particular situation.

Here, again, we have an antinomy similar to that which we have described at the borderline between the aesthetic and the extra-aesthetic. There we found an opposition between the complete absence of the aesthetic function and its presence. Here it exists between the subordination and the domination of the aesthetic function in the hierarchy of functions. Thus the aesthetic area is not torn apart into two mutually impenetrable segments, but rather it resembles a whole which is influenced by two opposing forces which simultaneously organize and dis-organize it. That is, they maintain within it a continuing course of development. If we consider art from this point of view its main task—the constant renewal of

[5] Let me add to this statement, and to several of those which precede it, that we must distinguish cases of particular exceptions resulting from the psychological dispositions of individuals from the case of collective postulation of the dominance of some extra-aesthetic function. Some observers, for instance, value the novel only insofar as it is educational or arouses the emotions. They evaluate a picture only as information about reality. For observers of this type, however, the work of art does not function as art, but as something either totally extra-aesthetic or else as having merely aesthetic coloration. Their view of art is inadequate and cannot constitute the norm.

a wide range of phenomena—becomes quite clear. This point will be discussed in more detail in the second chapter of this study where we will treat the aesthetic norm.

It is impossible to establish once and for all what is art and what is not. We introduced above some examples of gradual transition or oscillation between the provinces of art and that which lies outside of art. Now we shall attempt a detailed enumeration of systematically arranged examples in order to demonstrate more graphically the numerous and varied aspects, within this transition area, of the opposing forces which control the development and state of the aesthetic domain.

1. Some types of art are members of a continuous series in which we also find phenomena which are extra-artistic, and even extra-aesthetic. We have already introduced architecture as one example of this situation. Literature, too, is in the same position. In architecture there is a competition between aesthetic and practical functions (e.g., protection against changes in weather), while in literature the competition is between the aesthetic and the communicative functions. One could introduce an entire group of linguistic phenomena which inhabit the borderline between communication and art, we are speaking of oratory. The basic purpose of oratory, especially in its most typical forms—political eloquence and sermons—is to influence the convictions of an audience, and its most effective linguistic environment is emotional language (intended for the expression of feelings). Since, however, emotional language—as an established component of the language system—often supplies poetry with formal devices,[6] oratory may easily shift,

---

[6]Some linguists, C. Bally among them, equate, incorrectly, poetic language with emotional language, overlooking the fundamental difference between a self-referential phenomenon (poetry) and one that is communicative (aimed at emotions).

especially in some of its forms and in some periods of its development, so far into the area of poetry that it will be understood and evaluated as art. There are, conversely, types and periods of development which emphasize the communicative character of oratory. The essay is an example of the oscillation between poetry and communication. It is even possible to introduce in this connection several types of verse itself, in which the basis is just this struggle for supremacy between the aesthetic and the communicative functions. These are, for example, didactic poetry and the biographical novel. Note, too, that the boundary line between verse and artistic prose is determined to a great extent by the greater participation of the communicative function (extra-aesthetic) in prose as compared to poetry. The reign of the aesthetic function is not absolute in any type of art. Drama oscillates between art and propaganda; the history of the productions by the Czech National Theater vividly illustrates that extra-aesthetic motives were the decisive ones, namely: the need for nationalistic propaganda. The dance as an art is closely related to physical training which has a hygenic function, and includes such forms as the Dalcrose school, where physical training has completely merged with the dance. Additionally, it often happens in the dance that other functions—religious (ritual dances) and erotic—operate in strong competition with the aesthetic function.

Let us now turn to visual arts other than architecture, namely to painting and sculpture. Here, too, there exist, completely outside the realm of art, creations which are purely communicative, e.g., pictures and models used in the study of the natural sciences. There are also cases in which the aesthetic function is secondary to some other, dominant function, e.g., maps as decorative objects, and finally, instances which are exactly on the borderline between art and total extra-aesthetics; painted, graphic and plastic advertising. The poster is in the extra-artistic category, since its primary goal is publicity. It is also possible, however, to study the history of the poster as an art form. There is, finally, a branch of painting and sculpture which is entirely artistic, but which nevertheless contains an oscillation between communicative and self-centered functions. This is the portrait, which is simultaneously a depiction of a person that we judge by criteria of physical resemblance, and an artistic creation having no necessary connection with reality. The portrait thus differs functionally from a painting which is not a portrait, even though the latter may realistically portray a likeness of its model. Now let us turn to music, in which one finds the fewest direct contacts with the extra-aesthetic realm. This is due to the particular nature of musical material—tone. Being necessarily understood as part of a tonal system, it already has an aesthetic coloration; cf. the well-known novella by Grillparzer: *"Der arme Spielmann,"* whose hero achieves an aesthetic ecstasy by constantly repeating one and the same note. One can, however, find cases in which the aesthetic function is only an accompanying function and not a dominant one. These are, e.g., melodic signals (military, etc.), and semi-sung outbursts of advertising (in train stations or on the streets) whose main purpose is to call attention to commercial products. An oscillation between the dominance of the aesthetic function and of other functions occurs, for example, in march music or in work songs. In national and state anthems the aesthetic function must compete with a symbolic function, and hence with a variant of the communicative function. We should also note the multiplicity and oscillation in function of musical folklore, although we cannot treat it here in any detail.

2. We have selected cases in which art enters into extra-artistic and even extra-aesthetic phenomena. Now let us observe some opposite situations. There are some phenomena which are basically rooted outside of the aesthetic realm, but which tend toward art without wholly becoming art, e.g., motion pictures, photography, ornamentation, or horticulture. The most obvious tendency toward art occurs in films. In some of its aspects the film is closely related to several art forms, namely: epic poetry, drama and painting. In various stages of its development it actually has approached one or another of these forms. Furthermore, there is evidence that it may become an autonomous art form with its own means for achieving dominance of the aesthetic function. Chaplin is creating a type of film hero which is completely different from stage heroes (mimicry and gestures for close-ups). Russian directors such as Eisenstein, Vertov and Pudovkin are perfecting the use of specifically filmic space whose third dimension is provided by the mobility of the camera. On the other hand, and more importantly, the film is an industry. As a result its supply and demand are determined by purely commercial considerations to a greater extent than is the case in any of the arts. This is also the reason why the film must—like any other industrial product—instantly and passively absorb every newly discovered improvement of its technological basis. In this respect it is sufficient to note the deliberate selectivity evinced by music which—in certain periods of its development—chooses, from among a number of technical possibilities available at the time, a limited number of instruments for particular artistic aims, and to compare this approach with the rapid tempo of innovation in talking motion pictures, which have in very brief time destroyed the bases for artistic development established by the

silent film. Although motion pictures are constantly striving to become art, it is still too early to say that they have entered a stage in which the aesthetic function is *de jure* the dominant one. The situation is somewhat different in the case of photography, which alternates between self-orientation and communication, but this condition we feel to be part of its very nature. Originally photography was seen as a new painting technique (cf the epigram *"Daguerreotype"* by Havlíček: "The painters have brought some things forth,/But they have not brought the light to light,/so the light grew angry at them/and began to paint by itself.") and in fact it was mainly used by professional painters and it adopted, for instance, the compositional devices of painting. In time, the photograph, in the hands of professional photographers, became extra-aesthetic and purely communicative. "Photograph" and "picture" acquired contradictory meanings. As a result of Impressionist painting, artistic photography (especially by amateurs) is drawing closer to painting. It has finally realized its particular destiny which is to occupy a borderline. It is characteristic of this oscillatory behavior of photography that its basic, or at least one of its most important genres, is the portrait, which it has employed throughout its existence, and the portrait, as we have noted above, is based on the thesis of oscillation.

So-called applied art has a different relation to art than does photography. This term we understand to mean a historical phenomenon existing at the end of the nineteenth and the beginning of the twentieth centuries, and not such enduring crafts as that of goldsmith, etc., which are usually mentioned in handbooks on the history of art. These crafts, involved as they were with the production of items for daily use, always had, in the majority of their subdivisions, a certain aesthetic coloration, and were even in close external contact with art (cf. the painter's guild as one aspect of craft organization). A mutual relationship completely different from mere parallelism, however, was formed when so-called decorative art arose. Here, craftsmanship attempted to exceed its boundaries and to transform itself into art in an effort to preserve handicrafted products which were losing their practical significance in competition with factory-produced goods. The atrophied aesthetic function was supposed to replace the lost practical functions of the craft, since these latter were better performed by industrial production. Art, which welcomed the rise of decorative art (cf. the fate of artist-designers), renewed its contacts with substances, in the material sense of the word, such as wood, stone, metal, etc., for art (especially architecture, which was closest to the crafts) had lost, in the rapid development of production technology, a feeling for materials. It only admitted new materials as substitutes for other ones, ignoring their specific properties, and it finally resulted in out-and-out violation of materials: viz. Secessionist architecture. Theoretically the path to decorative art was paved by this very same analysis of the materials employed in art: viz. *Der Stil* by G. Semper which appeared in the years 1860-63. For quite practical reasons the properties of materials (e.g. strength) are basic considerations in the crafts. As a result the crafts were to contribute to the growing use of the creative possibilities offered by various materials. When decorative art had completely entered the field of art, i.e., had begun to attempt to create unique products in which the aesthetic function predominated, it lost its practical function. It began to turn out vessels from which it would be "a shame" to drink, furniture which would be "a shame" to use, etc. Soon it began to produce glasses from which it was difficult to drink, etc.

This loss of practical functions in the crafts is brilliantly revealed in the anecdote by Loos about the harness-maker:[7] There once was a harness-maker who made exceedingly serviceable saddles. But he wanted his saddles to be modern at the same time. He went to a professor of art who told him the principles of decorative art. Following these principles, the harness-maker attempted to make a perfect saddle, but it turned out just like the ones he had always made. The professor accused him of a lack of imagination, had some plans drawn up by his students, and even drew several himself. When the harness-maker saw the plans he rejoiced and said to the professor: "Professor, if I had as little understanding of horseback riding, the properties of leather and craftsmanship as you do, I would have as much imagination as you do." Decorative art was to a certain extent an anomaly, albeit a necessary and normal fact of evolution in aesthetics. A fleeting glance at it has shown us a new aspect of the dialectical connection between art and the sphere of extra-artistic aesthetic phenomena.

From the examples which we have enumerated above there still remains the relationship between art and horticulture. Horticulture, whose actual goal is the cultivation of plants, approaches art, even becomes art, when architecture wishes to adapt nature to the builders' creations. Hence we note the particularly forceful sweep of horticulture as an art in the Baroque and Rococo eras, when castle construction required its assistance (*Le Notre* in Versailles). In our times the urbanistic concept of including an entire city in a unified scheme involves the participation of horticulture; viz., e.g., the *"Ville radieuse"* of Le Corbusier: "houses and skyscrapers on pillars, returning all the earth to

[7]*Trotzdem,* Innsbruck, 1931, p. 15n.

traffic, especially pedestrian traffic. The entire surface of the city becomes a park."[8]

3. Finally we add a remark on two special cases which we place in the same category not by virtue of their relatedness—they are not related—but due to their difference from the cases introduced above in 1 and 2. These are religious ceremonies and the beauty of nature (especially landscapes) as they relate to art. It is well-known that religion contains, as a rule, a considerable amount of aesthetic elements; in many religions the aesthetization of ceremony has proceeded so far that art has become an integral part of them (cf. Catholic and Orthodox church art). Often the ceremony is so saturated by the aesthetic function that theoreticians do not hesitate to call it an art form, especially in periods where the specifically religious aspect of the ceremony is weakened (e. g., the rebirth of religiosity among romantics like Chateaubriand in the period of atheism which existed during the French Revolution). The religious function is, however, always the dominant aspect of the ceremony as far as the church is concerned. If it nevertheless admits art as an integral element of the ceremony, it does so with the stipulation that the basic principles of ceremony be subjected to outside directives, to norms which involve not only subject matter but also artistic structure (e.g., the blue garment of the Virgin in the Middle Ages). The intention of these stipulations is to place barriers in the path of the aesthetic function, even though they should not entirely suppress it or subjugate it, but should only create from it a twin having some other function. One can say that in church art (and to a certain extent in the entire area of related activities) there exist simultaneously *two dominant functions*, one of which, the religious one, makes of the

[8]K. Teige: *Nejmenší byt,* Prague, 1932, p. 142.

other—the aesthetic one—the means of its own realization. We refer here to a kind of contamination rather than a functional hierarchy. As concerns medieval religious art, we must bear in mind that the milieu from which that art sprang was unaware—like today's folk milieu—of any clear mutual differentiation of individual functions. The second case which we wished to discuss was landscape beauty. Nature is an extra-aesthetic phenomenon, providing it has not been touched by a human hand guided by aesthetic intent. In spite of this, however, the countryside can serve as a work of art. The solution to the problem as it was stated e.g., by Hostinský[9] and as it was clearly formulated by C. Lalo[10] is simple: "In the souls of cultivated persons art is reflected in nature and imparts its brilliance to nature." Here the dominance of the aesthetic function has been introduced from without.

The examples which have been assembled in the foregoing paragraphs have had a single purpose: a demonstration of the variety of transitions between art and the spheres of extra-aesthetic as well as extra-artistic aesthetic phenomena. It became apparent that art is not a closed territory. There is no strict boundary or unambiguous criterion which would separate art from that which is outside of art. An entire group of products may occupy the borderline between art and other aesthetic or extra-aesthetic phenomena. In the course of its development art constantly alters its province, sometimes broadening, sometimes contracting it. Despite this—or rather because of it—the polarity between the dominance and subordination of the aesthetic function in the functional hierarchy maintains its

[9]O. Hostinský: *Co jest malebné?*, Prague, 1912.
[10]*Introduction à l'esthétique*, Paris, p. 131.

undiminished validity. Without the assumption of this polarity, development within the sphere of aesthetics would lose its meaning, since it is just this polarity which provides the dynamics of continuous evolutionary change.

Summarizing our remarks on the distribution and influence of the aesthetic function, we may draw the following conclusions: 1. The aesthetic is, in itself, neither a real property of an object nor is it explicitly connected to some of its properties. 2. The aesthetic function of an object is likewise not totally under the control of an individual, although from a purely subjective standpoint the aesthetic function may be acquired (or, conversely, lost) by anything, regardless of its organization. 3. Stabilizing the aesthetic function is a matter for the collective and is a component in the relationship between the human collective and the world. Hence any given distribution of the aesthetic function in the material world is tied to a particular social entity. The manner in which this entity deals with the aesthetic function predetermines, in the final analysis, both the objective organization of objects intended to produce an aesthetic effect and the subjective aesthetic reaction to those objects. Thus, for example, in periods when the collective tends toward intensive use of the aesthetic function, the individual is more free to relate aesthetically to objects, either actively (in creating them) or passively (in perceiving them). The tendencies to widen or narrow the aesthetic realm, since they are social facts, always manifest a number of attendant symptoms. In this sense, poetic Symbolism and Decadence, with their panaestheticism, are parallel to and synonymous with modern applied art, which is expanding the boundaries of art to excess. All of these phenomena are symptomatic of the extreme hypertrophy of the aesthetic function within a contemporaneous social context. A similar set of parallel phenomena may be observed today. Modern (Constructivist) architecture is tending, in theory and practice, to abandon artistic features and proclaims its ambition to become a science, or, more precisely, an application of scientific concepts, and of sociological concepts in particular. Surrealist poets and artists are approaching the problem from a different direction. They base their approach on scientific research into the subconscious. So-called Socialist Realism in literature, particularly in Russian literature, belongs in part to this category since it requires of art, first and foremost, the synthetic depiction and propagation of a new social order. The common denominator of these varied and sometimes partially inimical tendencies is the polemic versus "artistry" which was so much emphasized in the recent past, i.e., a reaction to the realization of absolute supremacy of the aesthetic function in art—a reaction which is expressed by the current tendency of art to approach the realm of extra-aesthetic phenomena.

The aesthetic sphere develops as a whole and is, in addition, constantly related to those aspects of reality which, at a given point in time, do not exhibit the aesthetic function at all. Such unity and integrity are possible only if we assume a collective awareness which combines the ties among objects bearing the aesthetic function and which unifies mutually isolated individual states of awareness. We are not postulating collective awareness as a psychological reality,[11] nor does this term indicate simply the total import of a group of social components to individual states of consciousness.

---

[11] The rather unfortunate term "collective awareness" could lead to this erroneous interpretation.

Collective awareness is a social fact. It can be defined as the locus of existence of individual systems of cultural phenomena such as language, religion, science, politics, etc. These systems are realities even though they can not be perceived by the senses. They reveal their existence by exerting a normative influence on empirical reality. Thus, for example, any deviation from a linguistic system embedded in the collective awareness is spontaneously noted and is evaluated as a mistake. The aesthetic also appears in the collective awareness, primarily as a system of norms. We will treat this point in Chapter II.

Collective awareness should not, however, be understood abstractly, i.e., without considering the concrete collective in which it is manifested. This concrete collective, this social unit, is internally differentiated into strata and *milieux*. It would be inconceivable for that which we call its awareness to be independent of these differences in society. The same holds true for the aesthetic realm. Art itself presents a number of complicated sociological problems, although the domination of the aesthetic function and the considerable autonomy which result from it isolate art to a great extent from reality and exclude it from direct contact with forms and tendencies of social intercourse (cf. the well-known formula in Kant: *"das interesselose Wohlgefallen"*). This is even more true of the aesthetic area which primarily interests us here. It is involved in an entire system of social morphology and is present in social activities.

It will be most convenient to ascertain the relationship between the aesthetic realm and the concrete arrangement and life of the social entity in our investigation of aesthetic norms in Chapter II. Let us add to the sociology of aesthetics a few notes from the standpoint of the aesthetic function:

1. The aesthetic function can cause social differentiation in cases where a certain thing (or act) has an aesthetic function in one social context while having none in a different context, or where it has a weaker function in one than in another. Note, for example, the statement by P. Bogatyrev (*Germanoslavica,* II) that the Christmas tree, which has primarily an aesthetic function in cities, functions mainly as ritual magic in the eastern Slovak countryside to which it migrated from the cities as a *"gesunkenes Kulturgut."*

2. The aesthetic function as a factor in social intercourse operates by means of its basic characteristics. Foremost among these basic characteristics, is the property which E. Utitz[12] designates as the ability to *isolate* an object by means of the aesthetic function. In a related concept, aesthetic function causes maximal focus of attention on a given object.[13] Wherever in social intercourse it becomes necessary to emphasize any act, object or person, to focus on it, to free it from undesirable associations, the aesthetic function emerges as an accompanying factor; cp. the aesthetic function of any ceremonial (including religion) or the aesthetic coloration of public celebrations. Due to its isolating properties, the aesthetic function can also become a socially differentiating factor; cp. the greater sensitivity toward the aesthetic function, and its more intensive utilization, in the higher levels of society which attempt to distinguish themselves from the other social levels (the aesthetic function as a factor in "prestige"), or the deliberate use of the aesthetic function to stress the

---

[12] *"Philosophie in ihren Einzelgebieten,"* Aesthetik und Philosophie der Kunst, p. 614.

[13] L. Rothschild: "Basic Concepts in the Plastic Arts," *The Journal of Philosophy,* XXXII, 1935, part 2, p. 42.

importance of people in power, as well as to separate
them from the rest of the collective (e.g., the clothing
of the actual people in power or of their subordinates,
their residences, etc.). The isolating power of the aesthetic function—or rather its ability to direct attention
to an object or a person—makes it an important concomitant factor in the erotic function. Note, for example, clothing, especially women's clothing, in which these
two functions often merge completely.

Another important feature of the aesthetic function is the pleasure which it evokes. Hence its ability to
facilitate acts to which it belongs as a secondary function, as well as the ability to intensify the pleasure connected with them; cp. the use of the aesthetic function
in child-rearing, dining, housing, etc. Finally we must
mention a third, unique property of the aesthetic function, conditioned by the fact that this function attaches
above all to the *form* of an object or act; it is the ability
to supplant some other function which the item (object
or act) has lost in the course of its development. Hence
the frequent aesthetic coloration of relics, either material (e.g., ruins, folk dress in areas where its other functions—practical, magical, etc.—have vanished), or nonmaterial (e.g., various rituals). It is appropriate here to
mention the well-known fact that the same process often
occurs with scientific works which, in the period of their
origin, possessed both an intellectual and a concomitant
aesthetic function. The works outlived their scientific
validity and went on to function partially or entirely
aesthetically—cf. *Dějiny* by Palacký or the works of
Buffon. An aesthetic function which supplants other
functions often causes cultural conservatism in the sense
that it preserves for a future period human products and
institutions which have lost their original, practical function, so that they can again be used, this time in a different practical function.

Thus the aesthetic function means much more than mere coating on the surface of an object or of the world, as some people would have us think. It significantly affects the lives of individuals and society, shares in the organization of contacts —active as well as passive—of individuals with that reality in which they find themselves. The remainder of this article will be devoted, as we noted above, to a more detailed examination of the social importance of aesthetic phenomena. This introduction was an attempt to delimit the aesthetic realm and to explore the nature of its developmental dynamics.

## II

Chapter I attempted to point out the dynamics of the aesthetic function, both in relation to phenomena which exhibit it and to the society in which it occurs. Chapter II will attempt to treat the aesthetic norm in the same manner. If it was not difficult to demonstrate the changeability of the aesthetic function—regulated, of course, by the process of evolution—which *ex definitione* takes the form of energy, it is less easy to discover the dynamics of the aesthetic norm, which exists as a law striving for unchanging validity. The function as a living force seems preordained to be constantly altering the location and direction of its course whereas norms, rules, and degrees appear by their very nature to be static. Aesthetics arose in the past as the science of laws regulating sense perception (Baumgarten). For a long time its only goal seemed to be the investigation of universally binding conditions of beauty whose validity was derived from premises which were metaphysical or at least anthropological. In the latter case aesthetic value and its unit of measure, the aesthetic norm, were understood as basic properties of man, resulting from his very nature. Experimental aesthetics, as founded by Fechner, began with the axiom that there exist universally necessary conditions for the existence of beauty, and that to ascertain them it is sufficient to isolate, through a number of experiments, the chance deviations of individual taste. As we know, further development forced experimental aesthetics to respect the changeability of norms and to take into account their bases. In other branches and directions of modern aesthetics there arose a mistrust of the unrestricted force of norms. In the majority of these new directions one found either skepticism concerning the very existence and validity of the norms, or at least an attempt to limit validity to each individual situation (the norm derived from the person of the artist), or finally, a tendency to preserve the overall force of the norm through empirical deduction of criteria from existing works presumed to be exemplary models. Such an approach must confront either incomplete induction or *petitio principii.*

We will not attempt to criticize particular solutions, but will try to oppose to all of them the positive argument that the disagreement between the requirement that the norm have overall validity—without which there would be no norm—and its actual limitation and variability are not contradictory, but can be theoretically grasped and mastered if we see them as forming a dialectical antinomy which promotes development in the entire area of aesthetics. The main body of our argument will concern the connections between the aesthetic norm and social organization, for both the changeability of the norm and its force cannot be equally grasped and justified either from the standpoint of mankind as a type, or of men as individuals, but only by considering man as a social product. But before we move on to the actual sociology of the aesthetic norm, we must introduce several fundamental concepts by the use of a noetic analysis of the essence of the norm.

Let us begin with a general consideration of value and norm. We accept the teleological definition of value as the ability of something to assist in the attainment of some goal. Naturally, the establishing of the goal and the striving toward it depend on some individual, and thus in every value judgement there exists a degree of subjectivity. In extreme cases the individual values something from the standpoint of a totally unique goal. In this event the value is not governed by any laws and depends entirely on an independent decision by the individual. The act of evaluation is less isolated in cases when, although its result is still valid only for a single person, nonetheless it involves a goal known to a person from prior experience. Here the evaluation can be guided by one rule whose force is determined in every given instance by the individual himself. Thus here, too, the decision depends, in the final analysis, on the independent will of the individual. We can only speak of a real norm when we have a publicly acknowledged goal with respect to which value is perceived as existing independently of the will of an individual and his subjective decisions. In other words, it must exist as a fact of the so-called collective awareness. This category includes, among others, aesthetic value, which provides dimensions to aesthetic pleasure. In such situations value is stabilized by a norm, by a general rule which can be applied to every concrete case which is subject to it. The individual may disagree with this norm or even attempt to change it, but he can not deny its existence or its collective validity while he is performing his value judgement—albeit one which differs from the norm.

Although the norm strives to attain universal validity, it can never achieve the force of a natural law—otherwise it would become one itself, and cease to be a norm. If, for example, man were unable to overstep the boundaries of absolute rhythm—as he is unable to see infra-red and ultra-violet radiation—rhythm would change from a norm which requests fulfillment but which need not be realized, into a law of the human organism which is adhered to of necessity and unconsciously. Thus the norm, although it attempts to attain universal validity, limits itself by this same attempt. Not only can a norm be violated, but it is possible—and happens often in actual practice—to have a parallelism of two or more norms which apply to a single concrete instance, measure the same value and are in mutual competition. The norm is thus based on a fundamental dialectical antinomy between universal validity and mere regulative or even orientational potential which implies that its violation is conceivable. Every norm has this two-fold, contradictory tendency between whose poles its development takes place. Nevertheless the various types of norms gravitate unequally to one pole or the other. The difference in gravitation becomes clear if we contrast, for example, a juridical norm which, in its usual meaning of "law," tends to absolute validity, with the aesthetic norm, especially in its most specific application as an artistic norm serving, usually, as a mere background to constant violation.

Nevertheless the aesthetic norm can exhibit a tendency toward unchangeable validity. In the development of art there appear, from time to time, periods which insist on constant and universal validity of a norm. As examples let us consider French Classical poetry and Symbolist poetry. Belief in the force of the norm was so strong during the Classical period that Chapelain could write in the foreword to his epic work *La Pucelle:* "In working out my theme I employed only a proper aware-ness of what was required. . . . It was merely an attempt to discover whether that genre which had been con-demned by our most famous writers was really dead, or whether the theory of the genre, which I knew quite well, could enable me in practice to demonstrate to my friends that without a great spiritual soaring it is possi-ble to use it successfully."[14] Translated into our termi-nology this statement expresses the unequivocal belief that correct application of a norm is itself sufficient to create artistic value. Concerning Symbolism, it is suffi-cient to recall the desire to create an "absolute work" which has prevailed regardless of period or milieu, and which appeared so intensively in, for example, Mal-larmé.[15] We can introduce, as additional evidence of the tendency of the aesthetic norm to become absolutely binding, the mutual intolerance of competing aesthetic norms which is often brought to light in polemical situ-ations. The aesthetic norm is replaced by another, more authoritative norm—e.g., a moral norm—and one's op-ponent is called a deceiver, or else by an intellectual norm, in which case the opponent is called ignorant or stupid. Even when the right of the individual to make aesthetic judgements is emphasized, one hears in the same breath the request for responsibility for them: indi-vidual taste is a component of the human value of the person who exercises it.

---

[14]F. Brunetière: *L'évolution des genres (Deuxième lecon).*
[15]Cf. the introduction to *Žalmy* (Prague, 1934) by Hlaváček, which presents a noetic characterization of Symbolism.

Thus the antinomy of unlimited binding force and its negation, constant change, hold true also for the aesthetic norm even if the apparent negation predominates. Here too, as everywhere else, every member is a starting point from which we must proceed in the analysis of a specific type of aesthetic norm. We must thus pose the question of whether there actually exist some sort of aesthetic principles resulting from the human organism itself, and thus inherent in man, which would justify the tendency of the aesthetic norm toward legal validity. We have already noted that the original concept of experimental aesthetics foundered in an attempt to establish such a principle. The difference between our idea and that of original experimental aesthetics lies in the fact that with regard to the latter the principles were postulated as ideal norms whose exact definition and observance could guarantee aesthetic excellence, whereas for us they are merely anthropological hypotheses for the thesis of a dialectical antinomy of the aesthetic norm—a thesis whose equal antithesis is the maintenance (and hence destruction) of constitutive principles.

The aim of the aesthetic function is the evocation of aesthetic pleasure. We have already mentioned in the previous chapter that any object or action, regardless of how it is organized, could acquire an aesthetic function and thus become objects of aesthetic pleasure. But there are certain pre-conditions in the objective arrangement of an object (which bears the aesthetic function) which facilitate the rise of aesthetic pleasure. Aesthetic potential is not inherent in an object: In order for the objective pre-conditions to be effective, something in the arrangement of the subject of aesthetic pleasure must correspond to them. Subjective presuppositions can be motivated by the individual, or society, or, finally, anthropologically, that is, by the very nature of man as a species. And it is precisely these anthropological conditions which concern us. Any number can be enumerated. They are, for example, for the temporal arts (Zeitkünste) —rhythm, based on the regularity of blood circulation and breathing (note, also, that people are most satisfied with rhythmically organized labor); for spatial art—vertical and horizontal, right angle, and symmetry which can be derived entirely from the structure and usual positionings of the human body;[16] for painting—the complementarity of colors and several phenomena of color and intensity contrast;[17] and for sculpture—the law of the stability of the center of gravity. From these principles we can directly derive several others. From the law of symmetry, for example, we obtain the basic composition of enclosed space by a point lying at the intersection of diagonals (absolute symmetry). There are further principles which—even if their ties with the anthropological are much less clear than in those named above— nevertheless cannot be treated as though they do not exist: the golden mean, for instance. As the direct superstructure of constitutive principles we must postulate some previously conventional norms which, by virtue of long periods of familiarity, have now the property of being self-evident, tolerating deformation while not vanishing into the background (cf., e.g., the repertoire of consonances in octave music which, as we know, increased with the gradual development of music). The enumeration of anthropological principles which we

[16]Cf. A. Schmarsow: *Grundbegriffe der Kunstwissenschaft,* Leipzig-Berlin, 1905, and G. Semper: *"Ueber die formelle Gesetzmaessigkeit des Schmuckes als Kunstsymbol," Kleine Schriften,* Berlin-Stutgart, 1888, p. 326n.
[17]Cf., for example, Šeracký: *Kvantitativní určení barevného kontrastu na rotujících kotoučích,* Prague, 1923.

have provided above does not pretend to completeness. Even if it were complete, it is certain in advance that its network would not be so vast and dense as to contain the equivalents of all possible detailed aesthetic norms. In order to satisfy the hypothesis that the aesthetic norm as a whole is constitutively based, it is sufficient to discover ties between it and a psychophysical basis.

The question now arises, how do these principles function with respect to actual norms? To assume that they themselves are norms, ideal norms whose fulfillment within the realm of possibility necessarily implies artistic perfection, would mean the negation of the history of art. In the development of art not only are basic principles not, as a rule, observed, but on the contrary we see that periods which tend to observe them most closely are followed by periods of the greatest possible deviation. Periods of deformation, however weak or however radical, are actually more frequent, and one can not indiscriminantly label them as decadent. It is also characteristic that very exact adherence to anthropological principles leads to aesthetic indifference. Exact structural rhythm, symmetry of geometric figures, etc. are aesthetically indifferent. The great importance of the constitutive principles consists, however, in the fact that the great variety of aesthetic norms, as we see from a synchronic (static) cross-section, as well as from a diachronic (temporally dynamic) cross-section, always points to a single denominator, the psychophysical composition of man as a species. The principles are spontaneously functioning criteria for the conformity and discrepancy of concrete norms with regard to this composition. This is not to say that they limit the developmental changeability of norms, but that they are a solid basis with respect to which change can only be felt as the violation of order.[18] There cannot be a centrifugal, i.e. deformative, tendency unless an opposite, attracting, tendency is also demonstrated by constitutive principles. Šklovskij, who insisted that artistic deformation implies a maximum expenditure of energy,[19] is correct only if we assume that somewhere, as an implicit thesis, there exists a basic law of the conservation of energy. Otherwise deformation would cease to exist since it could not be a negation of regularity. And constitutive principles are in fact expressions of maximum conservation of energy in the realm of aesthetics.

In the preceding paragraphs we have attempted to provide a noetic explanation for the multiplicity of aesthetic norms (the coexistence of mutually competing norms). There still remains, however, a genetic explanation, i.e., how, in fact, this multiplicity arose. Thus it will be necessary to consider the aesthetic norm as a historical fact, i.e. to begin with its changes through time. This is a necessary result of its dialectical nature which was noted earlier. The aesthetic norm undergoes temporal change simultaneously with other types of norms. Every norm changes by virtue of the fact that it is constantly being re-applied, and it must adjust itself to new circumstances which arise as a result of these new applications. Thus, for example, linguistic norms—grammatical, lexical or stylistic—are constantly changing. The change is, however—except for linguistic forms which belong to the area of linguistic pathology, the so-called private languages—so slight as to be indistinguishable, so that the problem of linguistic changes is one of the most

[18]K. Teige: *"Neoplasticismus a suprematismus,"* Stavba a báseň, 1927, p. 114: "In principle we can find in architecture many substantial reasons to support asymmetry. But even so, symmetry must be admitted as a special case of asymmetry."

[19]*"Iskusstvo kak priem,"* O teorii prozy, Moscow-Leningrad, 1925.

difficult in linguistics. Because of the practical purpose
of language and because in its normal communicative
function language does not focus on verbal art, linguistic
norms are much more stable than aesthetic norms, but
nevertheless they do change. But norms which are even
more stable than linguistic norms undergo alterations
when applied to concrete material. This is true, for example, of legal norms, which by their very name of
"laws" indicate a tendency to unlimited and identical
application. Even Engliš[20] who tries to make a rigorous
distinction between mere deductive (normative) thinking and evaluatory (teleological) thinking, must state
that 'interpretation *per analogiam*' is not interpretation,
although it is necessary in solving cases which the law-
giver, while formulating a law, overlooked. In Engliš's
view, "interpretation *per analogiam* is simply a norm-
setting action, and legal forces thus contain special pow-
ers for making those interpretations which would not be
necessary if it were really only a matter of interpreting
existing norms."

Aesthetic norms are also transformed through application. If legal norms alter within very narrow limits—
and we are not including actual lawmaking—and linguistic norms change efficiently but invisibly, the transformations of aesthetic norms occur on a broader and more
obvious scale. Observance of the change of aesthetic
norms is not equally intensive in all branches of aesthetics; the most striking is in art, where violation of the
aesthetic norm is one of the primary means for achieving
an effect. Here we are on the threshhold of the evolution of artistic phenomena. Its problems are extensive
and intertwined with the influence of mutually related
individual problems. There is no space here to attempt a

---

[20]*Teleologie jako forma vědeckého poznání,* Prague, 1930.

detailed and systematic exposition,[21] but in view of all that we intend to present below we must say a few words about the process by which the aesthetic norm in art is transformed and multiplied.

A work of art is always an imperfect application of aesthetic norms. It destroys their previous form not through involuntary necessity but deliberately and hence, as a rule, very perceptibly. The norm is constantly being violated. We should note that, when examining the aesthetic norm from a developmental standpoint, we will employ the term "violation" in a different sense from that in which it was used above where we dealt with non-adherence to aesthetic principles. Here it will mean the relation between a chronologically prior norm and a new norm which is different from it, and which is in the process of being formed. The violation of constitutive principles by a concrete norm and the violation of an older norm by a newly-created norm are two different things. In evolution it must eventually happen that a norm similar to a corresponding constitutive principle (e.g., poetic rhythm which keeps strictly to the metrical scheme) will be felt as a strong violation if it was preceded by a period of conspicuous violation of that same principle: cf. the statement by a Russian poetic theoretician that it is possible to hear silence if it has been preceded by the sound of a gun shot. The history of art, if we examine it from the standpoint of the aesthetic norm, is the history of revolts against reigning norms. This explains the particular properties of living art— aesthetic pleasure and displeasure are both present in the impression which it makes on us. F. X. Šalda expressed this particular property very nicely: "The

---

[21] An outline was offered in my monograph on Polák's *Vznešenost přírody*, (1934).

impression which [a contemporary work of art] makes
on us is of something firm and exact . . . rather than of
something smooth and elegant—something which radically differs from the conventionality and pleasant indo-
lence of existing, customary artistic expression. . . .
Every true creator of art appears to well-trained experts
and navie amateurs alike to be crude. They speak of his
art as of something interesting, a curiosity, but his work
is not evaluated as a work of good taste and beauty."[22]
The term "good taste" which was used by Šalda brings
to mind one of the most radical violations of the aesthetic norm ever to be employed in art: the violation of
the norm with the aid of deliberately bad taste.

What is bad taste? Certainly it is not everything
which does not conform to the aesthetic norm of a given
point in the development of art. A broader concept than
"bad taste" is "ugliness." That which we see as not in
agreement with the aesthetic norm is, for us, ugly. We
only speak of bad taste when we evaluate an object produced by human hands and in which we observe a tendency to fulfill a certain aesthetic norm and which at the
same time lacks the ability to fulfill that norm. Natural
phenomena may be ugly, but not tasteless, except for
individual cases where they remind us of a human
product. The displeasure which a tasteless object arouses
is not based solely on the sensation of incongruence
with an aesthetic norm, but is strengthened by an aver-
sion to the helplessness of its creator. Thus bad taste
seems to be the most acute antithesis to art. Art, by its
very name, implies the ability completely to attain a
projected goal. But sometimes art employs bad taste in
order to attain its ends. A graphic example may be found
in the visual forms of Surrealist art which employ—as

[22] *"Nová krása, její geneze a charakter," Boje o zítřek.*

objects of representation and as components in montages (painting and plastic forms)—products from the period of the greatest decline in taste (the end of the nineteenth century), frequently factory imitations of art and handicrafts, illustrations by professional engravers from illustrated periodicals, etc. Thus is the norm of "lofty" art most radically violated and aesthetic displeasure most provocatively evoked as a component of artistic effect. The case of Surrealism was chosen for the striking manner in which the aesthetic norm was violated. Although in other periods and movements aesthetic displeasure is not flaunted so ostentatiously, it is almost always a part of living, developing art. If we would now pose the question of whether it is possible that art, a privileged aesthetic phenomenon, can evoke displeasure without ceasing to be art, the answer would be that aesthetic pleasure, if it is carried to maximum intensity—as happens in art—requires aesthetic displeasure as a counterbalance. Even when the norm has been most intensely violated, pleasure in art is still the dominant impression, and displeasure is a means for heightening it. It is no accident that Surrealist aesthetics in particular is intended to be hedonistic. Artistic value is indivisible. Even factors causing displeasure become, in the total work—but only there—positive elements. Outside of the work and its structure they would have negative values.

Thus the work of art always disturbs (sometimes slightly, sometimes considerably) an aesthetic norm which is valid for a given moment of artistic development. But even in extreme cases it must also adhere to the norm. Finally, there are periods in the history of art in which adherence to norms obviously predominates over violation of them. But there is always something in the work of art which is bound to the past and something which points to the future. As a rule the factors

involved are distributed among various groups of elements. Some observe the norm while others destroy it.
When a work of art first appears in public it can happen
that only those aspects will stand out which differ from
the past. Later, we always become aware of connections
with that which preceded the work in the evolution of
art. Manet's *Déjeuner sur l'herbe,* when it was first
shown, was opposed for being a revolutionarily novel
work. Only subsequent investigation revealed very clearly the strong ties to Manet's predecessor—Courbet—both
in composition and in the treatment of color.[23] Even
when a new artistic phenomenon is evaluated positively,
it is possible that at first—due to a strong impression of
violation of a former norm—the adherence to that norm
may be overlooked.[24]

A living work of art always oscillates between the
past and future status of an aesthetic norm. The present,
from which we observe the work of art, is felt as a tension between a former norm and its destruction, and the
destruction is intended to become part of a future norm.
As a very striking example let us take Impressionist
painting. One of the typical and basic norms of Impressionism is the tendency to present a direct sense perception not deformed by any intellectual or emotional interpretation. In this sense Impressionism is a correlate of
poetic Naturalism. At the same time, from the very be-
ginnings of Impressionism we can find a completely opposite tendency which, with the passage of time,
asserted itself ever more forcefully. This is the tendency
to destroy the concrete coordinates of sense data

[23]Cf. for example the detailed analysis by Deri in *Die Malerei im
XIX, Jahrhundert,* Berlin, 1920.

[24]This was pointed out, for example, by M. Hysek in regard to P.
Bezruč *(Tři kapitoly o Petru Bezručovi,* Brno, 1934).

concerning the depicted object. In this sense Impressionism, especially in its later development, is actually a partner of poetic Symbolism. The transition between opposing tendencies is made possible, in graphics, by annulling linear outline and hence linear perspective, and also by transferring outline into the spatial interplay of patches of color. And both of these opposing tendencies are classified by history under one label: Impressionism. This has always been true in the history of art. No developmental stage ever adheres completely to a norm which it adopted from a preceding stage, but rather it creates a new norm which destroys the old one. A creation which would totally observe an accepted norm would be standardized and repetitious. But only the work of imitative followers approaches this extreme, whereas a powerful work of art cannot be repeated and its structure is, as we noted above, indivisible, particularly with respect to the heterogeneity of the elements which it combines into a whole. As time passes, the feeling of dissonance—which was forcibly reconciled by the structure—disappears. The work becomes truly unified and also beautiful in the sense of aesthetic pleasure undisturbed by anything. F. X. Šalda was aware of this when he wrote: ". . . only the perspective of distance produces beauty."[25] Structure becomes divisible into individual details of the norm, and they can be applied, without harming them, outside the area of the structure in which they originated, and even completely outside of the realm of art. Whenever this process is accomplished, a developmental stage in art which was, up to that moment, topical, becomes an element of the historical heritage, while the norm which created it slowly penetrates the entire realm of aesthetics, either as a

---

[25] *"Nová krása, její geneze a charakter," Boje o zítřek.*

unified group (canon) or as isolated fragments (smaller groups or norms or individual, particular norms). Everything which we have said here regarding the creation of norms is valid, of course, in its entirety, only for one kind of art which, for lack of a better term, we will call "lofty." It is that art which is embraced (with restrictions which will be introduced below) by the dominant social stratum. Lofty art is the source and innovator of aesthetic norms. Other art forms coexist with it (e.g., salon, tabloid, and folk art, etc.), but they usually take over an altered norm from lofty art. In addition to art of all sorts there naturally exist, as we stated in Chapter I, extra-artistic aesthetic phenomena. So the question arises: How do aesthetic norms created by lofty art penetrate into *this* area?

At this point let us recall the discussion in the first chapter concerning the gradual nature of the transition between art and other aesthetic phenomena. F. Paulhan put it nicely ". . . great art such as painting or sculpture is, in one way, equal to the decorative arts: the purpose of a painting or a statue is to decorate a hall, salon, facade or fountain." One must add that, for Paulhan, decorative art is "that type of production which by processing some material gives it a useful form, or else is limited to decorating the material."[26] Thus, in the opinion of Paulhan, and of Frenchmen in general, decorative art is not true art but a craft, and hence a non-artistic aesthetic phenomenon. Paulhan indicated that the decorative and also the practical function can distort art from other areas beyond recognition. This was put more clearly by O. Hostinský: "If we attribute to architecture a portal with decorative doors, by what right do we place in a lower category a work, perhaps even by the

---

[26]*Mensonge de l'art*, Paris, 1907.

same person, such as a precious cabinet or some other piece of portable furniture?"[27] We find here one of the natural bridges between art and the remainder of aesthetics. There are, however, many other ways in which norms travel from the norm-setting area of lofty art into the extra-aesthetic realm.

Let us introduce another example—the influence of the theatrical gesture on the gesture found in the area of so-called good breeding. We know that "good breeding" in society is a fact which has a strong aesthetic coloration,[28] but its dominant function is different: to facilitate and regulate social encounters among members of a collective. This is an aesthetic fact which is extra-artistic, and the same can be said of gestures in the broadest sense of the word, including mimicry and linguistic phenomena such as intonation and articulation. In these latter the aesthetic function has the important task of suppressing the originally spontaneous expressiveness of the gesture and of turning a gesture-reaction into a gesture-sign. But we also note the following interesting fact: not only does a social gesture differ from one country to another (even if we take countries which have approximately the same level of culture and the same strata within them), but—sometimes radically— within one country in different periods. To prove this statement one has only to examine paintings and drawings (especially engravings) and photography from relatively recent times such as the 1840's and 1850's. The most conventional gesture, for example, such as standing upright, seems to us in these works to be overly emotional. The people thrust forward whichever foot is not

[27]*O významu průmyslu uměleckého,* Prague, 1887.
[28]Cf. in this connection M. Dessoir: *Aesthetik und allgemeine Kunstwissenschaft.*

bearing the weight of their bodies, their hands appear to express some emotion which is disproportionate to the situation, etc. Social gestures are thus subject to evolution. But what causes this evolution? Just as sense perceptions, especially visual and aural, alter under the influence of art (painting and sculpture enable man to perceive the act of seeing in a continually new way, and music has the same effect on hearing), just as poetry continually renews in man the awareness of speech as a creative relationship to language, in the same way gesticulation has a corresponding art which constantly renews it; it is the acting profession—found for centuries in the theater and recently in films as well. For an actor the gesture is an artistic fact with a dominant aesthetic function and consequently free of any context involving social relationships, and thus there is more freedom for alterations of gestures. The new norm which arises from an alteration penetrates backward from the stage to the audience. The influence of acting on the gesture has long been known to pedagogues and has led to the use of amateur acting as a pedagogical device (cf. school plays). Nowadays this influence is felt in daily life very strikingly, above all through the agency of the film. Before our very eyes in the space of a few years this influence has manifested itself, particularly among women, who are more imitative than men, in the entire system of gesticulation, from ambulatory gait to the most detailed motions such as opening a powder-box or the play of facial muscles. This is the way in which new aesthetic norms flow from art into daily life, whether the location is an artisan's workshop or a drawing-room. In the extra-aesthetic realm they acquire a validity which is more binding than in the art which gave birth to them, since they now function as an actual measure of value and not

merely as the setting in which violation of the norm may
be accomplished.

Even this application of norms is not entirely automatic, because it subjects the norm to the influence of
various forces such as fashions. Fashions are, basically,
not predominantly aesthetic phenomena, but are, rather,
economic; H. G. Schauer defines them as "the exclusive
domination which some product enjoys on the market
place for a certain period of time," and the German
economist W. Sombart devoted an entire study to the
economic aspect of fashions (Wirtschaft und Mode).
Nevertheless, among the numerous other functions of
fashion (such as the social, political, and, in dress, erotic
fashions) the aesthetic function is one of the most important ones. Fashion has a leveling effect on the aesthetic
norm in the sense that it eliminates the diverse competition of concurrent norms to the advantage of a single
norm; after World War I, together with the increased role
of fashion—at least in our part of the world—there was a
decrease in the difference between urban and rural dress
and between the dress of the older and younger generations. On the other hand, the leveling is compensated by
the rapid temporal alternation of norms which are due
to fashion. There is no need for examples, since one can
find plenty of them by leafing through a few fashion
magazine annuals. Extra-artistic aesthetic phenomena
comprise the natural environment of fashion, but sometimes it penetrates into art, especially into some of its
secondary branches such as salon or tabloid art, and here
it operates primarily in order to influence consumption;
cf. the vogue for pictures with particular themes as an
element of standardized household furnishings (still-life
paintings of flowers, etc.). It may happen that some actual works of art enter domestic living. Several years

ago *The Crucifixion* by Max used to hang in many homes.[29]

We have already stated that the source of aesthetic norms is lofty art, and that from such art they penetrate into other sectors of aesthetics. But the process is not so simple that norms can merely alternate as regularly as the waves which break on the sea shore, and where one wave arrives only when its predecessor has receded. Norms which have firmly implanted themselves into a given area of the aesthetic realm and into a given social milieu can last for a very long time. New arrivals move in to join them and the *co-existence and competition of numerous parallel aesthetic* norms occurs. There are cases, particularly in the folk culture, where aesthetic norms endure for entire centuries. It is well known, for example, that "as an architectionic form the (Czech) peasant adopted patterns based on late Renaissance and on Baroque principles; forms of urban and feudal attire in various periods of fashion from the beginning of the sixteenth century are basic for clothing and its ornamentation; the late Renaissance and the Baroque are the sources of ornamental decoration in painting, carving, embroidery and appliqué—and we have many examples of ornamental painting and carving from those periods."[30] In connection with Slovak folk embroidery. V. Pražák wrote that ". . . the Slovak country folk in the nineteenth and twentieth centuries still embroidered Renaissance ornaments just as they were introduced into

---

[29]Cf. also the study by H. G. Schauer: *Móda v literatuře* in which, while discussing the poetic theme of marital infidelity, he demonstrated, quite interestingly, that literary fashion, in contrast to fashion proper, is distinguished by inertia, and that fashion as a factor in poetic creation can hinder direct contact between literary and theatrical thematics and the actual state of society. The study was first published in *Moravské listy,* 1890, and reprinted in *Spisy H. G. Schauera,* Prague, 1917.

[30]*Ceskoslovenská vlastivěda,* VIII, Prague, 1935, p. 201.

men's fashions in the sixteenth and seventeenth centuries."[31]

We can also mention verses which lie on the borderline between folklore and poetry—inscriptions in the cemetery at Albrechtice (Písek) from the 1830's and 1840's—which employ not only syllabic versification but the entire poetics of Baroque poetry of the seventeenth and eighteenth centuries. This is attested, for example, by a parable on the potter's craft and God's creation, a typical poetic theme not only of the Baroque but also of medieval times. Another example is the naturalistic description in verse of the decomposition of the human body during an illness:

> The rotten flesh kept falling from her crippled legs,
> Until the bare bones could be seen.
> Her face was nearly covered with scabs.
> To add to her troubles she also became blind.[32]

We have only to compare this description with one which is authentically Baroque, e.g., from *"Píseň o smrti"* by Konias,[33] in order to ascertain that in the case of the Albrechtice inscriptions we are dealing with an actual remnant of the Baroque poetic canon which had survived to the period in which Mácha's *Máj,* the greatest creation in Czech Romanticism, originated and was published. In the first two examples which we have cited (Czech and Slovak folklore) the longevity of the norm is an indication of the penetration of the aesthetic norm and function into a rigid system of the most varied norms and functions, as is usually the case in folklore

---

[31]*Bratislava,* VII, p. 251n.

[32]Dating and citation according to R. Rožec: *Staré nápisy na náhrobních kapličkách na hřbitově v Albrechticích, Písek.*

[33]Cited by J. Vlček: *Dějiny české literatury,* II, 1, p. 56.

(cf. below on this subject), while in the third instance (cemetery inscription) the longevity is attested to by a fossilized poetic form, i.e., religious verse, which was already archaic when the inscription appeared.

We have introduced examples of outstanding survivals in the realm of aesthetic norms. Such cases are relatively uncommon and are possible only under special conditions. But the coexistence of older and newer norms is, in itself, a daily occurrence in aesthetics, and the norms are often in extremely close relationships. Thus, for example, if we examine contemporary Czech poetry we find, in addition to a structure which may roughly be defined as "post-war" (with the understanding that it is a conglomerate of several different canons, some already quite petrified), other canons. Among them are Symbolism and the Lumír group, and somewhere on the periphery, especially in children's verse, the *Máj* canon. Thus there are four groups of norms in existence simultaneously. In other types of art one could similarly point out several different canons which are being adhered to at the present time: all canons from Impressionism through Surrealism in painting, for example. A more reliable picture would be provided by statistics of consumption such as, e.g., library data on literature. The coexistence of different norms appears outside the world of art as well. We know that objects having an aesthetic function (furniture, clothing, etc.) are differentiated in production and distribution not only according to their material and intended use, but also on the basis of various tastes.

Thus a large number of aesthetic canons always exist simultaneously in any collective.[34] We know

---

[34]Cf. O. Hostinský in the brochure: *"O socializaci umění,"* Prague, 1903: "Among the common people—just as in the most affluent and

about them not only through objective experience, of which we have introduced several examples, but also from subjective experience. Just as each of us is able to speak several different forms of one and the same language, e.g., several social dialects, we also comprehend subjectively several aesthetic canons—cf. the above-mentioned cases in poetry—even if, as a rule, only one of them is completely adequate for us and is an element of our personal taste. But the coexistence of several different canons in the same collective is not without tension. Each of them strives for sole validity, and attempts to supplant the others. This follows from the claim of the aesthetic norm to be absolutely obligatory, as we mentioned above. The expansionist tendencies are especially noticeable where newer canons confront older ones. An entire aesthetic area is set in motion by such mutual exclusiveness. The incompatibility of different canons is also due to the fact, pointed out by G. Tarde,[35] that aesthetic norms, like moral norms, often have a negative character, i.e. they are formulated as prohibitions.

Aesthetic canons differ, as we have seen, in relative age. But this difference is not merely chronological, but is equally qualitative since older canons are more easily comprehended and face fewer obstacles which could bar

educated society—one single taste never reigns alone. Rather, a great variety of tastes prevail, and thus it is not possible to state the viewpoint of the common people *vis-a-vis* art in one universally valid formula. Such a doctrinaire approach is disproved by the most fleeting glance at theatrical repertoires, at the literary consumption in the broadest circles, at shops which sell pictures and paintings. Not only does this mixture contain a wealth of degrees from the worst to the best, but one also finds numerous historical strata superimposed one upon another, so that what appeals to various people today represents, on the whole, the evolution of art covering over a hundred years."

[35] *Les lois de l'imitation,* Paris, 1895, p. 375.

their acceptance. Thus it is possible to speak of an actual hierarchy of aesthetic canons whose apex is the newest canon, the one least automatic and the least involved with other types of norms. Lower down on the hierarchy we find canons which are older, more automatic, and more strongly anchored among other types of norms. (We will discuss below the relationship of the aesthetic norm to other norms.) It may seem that the hierarchy of aesthetic canons is directly related to the hierarchy of social strata. The latest norm, occupying the summit, seems to correspond to the highest social stratum, and in like manner further gradations of both hierarchies seem to have a mutual correspondence, so that lower social categories seem to correspond to older canons. As a rough outline this idea is not without some justification, but it should not be dogmatically understood as a valid blueprint of reality.

First of all let us not forget that, when considering the relation of social morphology to the aesthetic norm, both the division of society into strata (vertical division) and into age groups, sex and profession (horizontal division) are important.[36] All types of horizontal divisions can be effective in this connection. The generation division, for instance, may lead to a situation in which members of the same social stratum will have different tastes and that, conversely, members of different strata, but belonging to the same generation, may have very similar tastes. The differences in generations also cause most aesthetic revolutions in which new canons, or a shift from one social milieu to another, are involved. The division between the tastes of men and women is a familiar

---

[36]The divisions by age and sex are of course biologically caused, but in society they acquire social import. Physical age, for example, is not always a determining factor for membership in a given (social) generation.

phenomenon, and sometimes the aesthetic influence of women can appear to be conservative in comparison to that of men. Such is the case in folk culture. In other situations women are more progressive in their tastes: cf. L. Schücking on the family as a factor in the evolution of taste in English literature of the eighteenth century, where he examines the role of women in the appearance of the sentimental novel.[37] It is not at all necessary that the latest tastes be connected with the highest strata. In pre-war Austria, for example, and even more so in Russia, the leading social stratum was the aristocracy, but the champions of lofty art who produced new aesthetic norms were from the middle class.

Even so, the existence of a bond between aesthetic and social hierarchies is undeniable. Every social stratum, but also many environments (e.g. country—city), has its own aesthetic canon which is one of its most characteristic attributes. If, for example, an individual moves from a lower stratum to a higher one he tries, as a rule, at least to find the superficial characteristics of the tastes of that stratum to which he wishes to belong (an aesthetically motivated change in clothing, housing, social behavior, etc.). Since, however, a change of real personal tastes is a very difficult operation, spontaneous taste becomes one of the most hazardous, although often concealed, aspects of his original stratum. Whenever a tendency to regroup the social hierarchy arises in a particular collective, this tendency also affects the hierarchy of tastes. Thus, for example, the intensive development of socialistic attempts to eliminate class differences in the final decades of the nineteenth century was officially accompanied by the development of decorative arts, the establishment of folk theaters, and attempts at art

---

[37] *Die Soziologie der literarischen Geschmacksbildung*, Munich, 1923.

education. In Chapter I we discussed the close connections between the development of mechanization in industry and the revitalization of artisanship. But there
was also a connection with the tendencies of social evolution, and people were aware of it. One man who in-
spired an attempt to develop aesthetic culture, J. Ruskin,
saw himself as attempting to improve society (raising the
level of public morality, etc.), while his successors, W.
Morris and W. Crane, were socialistically motivated. At
the second Congress on Artistic Education, S. Waetzold
delivered a speech in which we find the statement:
"Even in its spiritual and social life the community is so
stratified and fragmented that one stratum scarcely un-
derstands another."[38] He anticipated a new unification
of society as the result of artistic education. These advo-
cates of artistic education, although operating from a
position which was unlike that of the Socialists, also
felt that art and aesthetic culture in general can serve as
social cement. Langbehn, the author of *Rembrandt als
Erzieher,* hoped to create out of the German peasants,
middle class and gentry *"eine Adelspartei im höheren
Sinne."* Hand in hand with the attempt to remove or at
least diminish the hierarchical nature of society there oc-
curred an attempt to equalize tastes, and on the highest
possible level: the newest and hence the highest aesthetic
norm was to become the norm of everyone.[39]

A continuation of this social and simultaneously
aesthetic effort took place at the start of the Russian

---

[38] This and the following quotation (Langbehn) are taken from J.
Richter: *Die Entwicklung des kunsterzieherischen Gedankens,* Leipzig,
1909.

[39] In this connection let us recall that L. N. Tolstoy in *What Is Art?*
also sought, with the aim of social equalization, the unification of the aesthetic canon, but in such a way that the upper levels of the aesthetic hierarchy would be rejected. He advocated universalization of the canons of
folk art.

revolution, when the artistic *avant garde* united with the social *avant garde*. But later in the Russian social transformation we find an attempt to discover an aesthetic equivalent to the classless society by reducing all tastes to the *average* level. Its symptoms are a compromised classicism in architecture, and Socialist Realism in literature in the form of a return to a slightly up-dated cliché of the realistic novel, and thus to an older canon which has already declined considerably. The relation between social organization and aesthetic norms is not, therefore, rigidly one-sided, even in the sense that a certain social tendency, e.g., the attempt to liquidate class divisions, always and everywhere had to reflect the same reaction in the area of aesthetics. There was an attempt to equalize canons on the highest level, another to promote universal acceptance of the average, and still another which suggested (cf. the reference to Tolstoy) a universal level in the sense of the archaization of the aesthetic norm to the lowest plane.

The relation between social organization and the development of the aesthetic norm is, as we see, undeniable and our schematic presentation of mutual parallelism of both hierarchies is not without justification. It becomes incorrect only if it is understood as an automatic necessity, and not merely as the basis for evolutionary variants. As it grows older and more rigid the aesthetic norm also sinks lower in the ranks of the social hierarchy. This process is, of course, complex, for no one social stratum is—because of the influence of horizontal divisions—an environment which is homogeneous in and of itself. Therefore we can, in a given stratum, distinguish several aesthetic canons. Even, for example, the domain of the ruling social stratum does not usually coincide with the domain of the newest aesthetic norm, even when this stratum has given birth to such a norm.

Supporters of the newest norm (both artists and the public) may be members of a younger generation which is in opposition—often not only aesthetic—to the older generation which actually is in power and which provides models for the lower strata. Or the supporters of the *avant garde* norm may be individuals who have come into conflict with the dominant stratum not by birth but by their upbringing and who themselves come from a lower stratum. Examples from Czech poetry would be Mácha and, several decades later, Neruda and Hálek.[40] In either case—whether it is a matter of rebellious youth, or members of alien strata—there appears at first in the dominating class itself a resistance to the new norm and only after such resistance subsides can the new norm become the norm of the social group which actually is dominant. And in the same manner it would be possible to analyze other strata with respect to the spread of aesthetic canons. There would be complications everywhere; one could hardly ever find an example of such firm ties between some aesthetic canon and a particular social formation that the canon would have exclusive rights within it or, conversely, would not exceed the boundaries of the formation. R. Jakobson and P. Bogatyrev provide an example of a canon which went beyond its native environment into another milieu:[41] in

---

[40] On the ties between the poetry of Mácha and his social origins cf. the article: *"Příspěvek k dnešní problematice básnického zjevu Máchova," Listy pro umění a kritiku,* IV. There are many passages in *"Hřbitovní kvítí"* which treat the manner in which the low social origins of Neruda are reflected in his poetry. The shock which greeted its appearance is well known. Interesting details of his subsequent gradual merger with the ruling stratum can be found in his correspondence with Světlá, published by A. Čermaková-Sluková (Prague, 1921). Neruda rebuked Světla, who had come from a middle-class Prague family, for behaving toward him like a "hofdáma." Světla characterized herself as the poet's "guvernantka."

[41] *"Die Folklore als eine besondere Form des Schaffens," Donum natalicium Schrijnen,* 1929.

Russian educated circles of the sixteenth and seventeenth centuries artistic literature and literary folklore (whose real home was the countryside) existed side by side. Despite all these complications, however, the concept of the sinking of an aging aesthetic norm down through various levels of the aesthetic and social hierarchies retains its validity.

Although it may decline, the aesthetic norm does not actually or irrevocably deteriorate, since as a rule it is not a matter of mere passive acceptance of a canon by a lower stratum, but of a certain active re-creation involving the aesthetic tradition of the given milieu and the entire group of norms of all types which are valid for this milieu. In addition it frequently happens that a canon which has sunk to the lowest periphery is suddenly elevated to the very center of aesthetic activity and becomes—in an altered form, of course—once again a new and vital norm. This is an especially frequent occurrence in contemporary art.[42] In this sense we could speak of the *rotation of aesthetic norms.*

There is one more important point which must not be forgotten in our attempt to define the sociology of the aesthetic norm. This is the relationship between the aesthetic norm and other norms. In our previous considerations we proceeded as if the aesthetic norm encountered the collective all by itself, and we disregarded the surroundings to which it was attached, i.e. we did not consider the total group of all types of norms which the given collective recognized as the criteria of various values. This approach was selected merely as a methodological restriction in order to simplify our presentation. Actually, however, there is no impenetrable wall between

---

[42]One may find examples in the study *"Dialektické rozpory v modernim umění," Listy pro umění a kritiku,* 1935.

the aesthetic norm and other norms. It is characteristic of their mutual proximity, for example, that the aesthetic norm can turn into some other norm, and *vice versa*. Thus, a moral norm, implemented in a novel by contrasting a good hero to an evil one, is transformed— as an element of poetic structure—into an aesthetic norm, and in time it becomes entirely a cliché which is totally independent of any current moral values, and may even be perceived in a comic light. In today's functional architecture, which denies any sort of aesthetic normative influence, practical norms (hygiene, etc.) become—even though the architect may not wish it— simultaneously aesthetic norms the minute the architect commences his work. One can also adduce examples of the opposite process, of aesthetic norms which become extra-aesthetic. In poetry, for example, there may occur a previously nonexistent linguistic phenomenon (e.g., a certain inversion in word order, or a certain lexicalization of a word group) which is done for aesthetic reasons, and which then might pass into non-poetic communicative language and thus become an element of the communicative linguistic norm. Some syntactical deformations in the works of Mallarmé became, in time, verbal tools of non-poetic literary speech, as the poet Cocteau has testified *(Le Secret professionnel):* "Nowadays Stéphane Mallarmé influences the style of the daily press even though the journalists do not suspect it."[43]

The close relationships between the aesthetic norm and other norms naturally facilitate their membership in the entire area of norms. Therefore when examining the ties between the aesthetic norm and the social

---

[43] On the transformation of the poetic aesthetic norm into an extra-aesthetic linguistic norm cf. also R. Jakobson: *"Co je poezie?," Volné směry*, XXX, p. 238.

organization we dare not overlook the fact that this is not a case of an isolated phenomenon encountering an isolated phenomenon (i.e. an aesthetic norm *vis-a-vis* a certain part of the collective). Rather, two entire systems are brought into mutual contact: the domain—or, still better, the structure—of norms, and the structure of the society for which the given norms form part of the collective awareness. The manner in which the aesthetic norm is connected with other norms forms part of their total structure and determines to a considerable extent their relation to social formations. In studying the sociology of the aesthetic norm it is necessary to pose two questions: the first concerns the closeness of its ties with other norms, the second its position—subordinate or dominant—among all norms. For differing social environments the answers to these questions will be different. Let us first examine the first of them—concerning the closeness of the penetration of the aesthetic norm among the others—and as an example we will juxtapose two types of normative contexts which correspond to two different social environments. On the one hand, we take a context valid for a social stratum which is culturally in the forefront and which creates cultural values and norms, and on the other, one which is valid for the social environment which contains the folklore culture. With respect to the question under consideration these environments are truly opposite.

The environment in which norms are created necessarily allows for a relatively free relationship between norms, for the freedom makes possible the intensive developmental motion of individual norms. Here the aesthetic norm most easily acquires that autonomy which isolates it from other norms. In this environment the artist's right, more or less acknowledged by society, to deform, in any area of art, other norms than aesthetic ones (e.g., moral) is related to the autonomy of the aesthetic norm. But such deformation is permitted only if the deformed norms function as components of artistic structure, and hence, aesthetically. Tabloid art, too, be it verbal or visual, willingly uses the aesthetic function to conceal other functions which are not tolerated by society. In freeing the aesthetic function from ties with other norms it is natural that the aesthetic norm should develop rapidly and with abrupt changes in direction. Conversely, in an environment which contains a truly undisturbed folk culture (as in our country, for example, the folk area near Carpathian Ruthenia, individual kinds of norms are tightly bound into a coherent structure, according to modern ethnographic investigators (cf. Lévy; Brühl, Durkheim, and especially the Russian ethnographer P. Bogatyrev on Carpathian Ruthenia). Because it is so tightly bound in the folk environment, the aesthetic norm fluctuates much less than it does in other environments and often endures for centuries with no appreciable alterations. Some ethnographers (the Naumann school) have made this fact the basis for the exaggerated thesis that "the folk do not produce, they only reproduce." What is true in this statement—as it relates to aesthetic norms—is the observation that the folk environment does not create its own norms, but takes them from the aesthetic realm—especially from the art—of the dominant social class. Therefore we can not say that aesthetic creativity is lacking in folk products. On the contrary, modern ethnography has shown that the difference between living folklore and industrialized production of folk objects (the folk art industry) lies precisely in the fact that industrial production is very schematized, while authentic folk creations (e.g., decoration and embroidery) possess infinite variations and nuances. This variety is, however, merely a number of variants of the norm, and not an evolutionary destruction of it. The stability of the aesthetic norm is made possible, as we have already seen, by its fixation within an entire system of norms. In the folk milieu norms are so closely interrelated that each prevents the others from changing.[44] This is the manner in which the folk environment differs so sharply from all others, and particularly from the milieu, mentioned earlier, in which cultural norms and values are created. Clearly this difference is also important in any social description of both of these social formations. It is also clear that the question of mutual interrelatedness of differing norm types is equally crucial for the sociology of the aesthetic norm.

We have already introduced another question which is relevant to the sociological evaluation of the ties between the aesthetic norm and other norms: in a given social environment does the aesthetic norm strive to dominate other norms or, conversely, does it tend to be subordinated in the total system of norms? Here, too, we will introduce as an illustration the confrontation of two types of environment. They are, first, the leading cultural milieu (the same as in the previous example), but here as seen in contrast to the non-folklore folk environment, i.e., to the urban folk situation as it has crystallized in our country with the growth of cities, especially large cities, in the first half of the nineteenth century. These two groups do not differ basically with respect to the merger of different types of norms. In both, the forces joining norms together are much freer

[44] Cf. the article by P. Bogatyrev: *"Příspěvek k strukturní etnografii,"* *Slovenská miscellanea,* Bratislava, 1931, in which he illustrates the point that "in ethnographic research we encounter facts having several functions, and often these various functions are so closely dependent upon one another that we are unable precisely to determine which function in a given situation is most strongly in evidence."

than in the folklore area. But there does exist between them a difference in the hierarchical order of the aesthetic norm. In that milieu which is in the cultural forefront—at least in contemporary society as we know from personal experience—the aesthetic norm easily gains ascendancy over other norms; cf. the waves of "art for art's sake" in art which, beginning in the nineteenth century, insistently recurred in the most varied movements within the world of art (e.g. in French literature: Flaubert and Realism, and soon thereafter among French Symbolists). Note, too, the simultaneous waves of panaestheticism outside of art. We are discussing, however, merely a tendency toward dominance of the aesthetic function, and not an actual and permanent domination. Occasionally, in fact, the attempts made to attain superiority of the aesthetic function encountered a resistance whose very intensity testifies to the strength of the forces against which it was reacting. Conversely, in the folk stratum the aesthetic function and the aesthetic norm are usually subordinated to other functions and norms, even in objects which can be designated as art: the aesthetic norm is not the paramount norm of that which J. Čapek termed "the most modest art." Its creative aspects were discussed by Čapek in a comparison with lofty art.[45] "Great statues and paintings elicit admiration by conveying in a superior fashion the beauty and power of the world and life. The most modest art, about which we wish to speak, also appeals to us. It simply wishes to show us things which are useful and necessary to man. It is imbued with a pious view of life and work, and knows the joy and necessity in both. It does not set itself lofty goals, but actualizes its modesty in a genuine and affecting manner, and thus performs a

[45] *"Malíři z lidu," Nejskromnější umění.*

considerable service. It wishes only to be an intermediary between items of daily use and mankind, but its language, poor and humble though it be, has a certain rare amiability and quiet warmth, and is natural and true." It is clearly stated here that in non-folklore popular art the aesthetic norm and function are subordinated to other norms, namely, utilitarian norms "to show us things which are useful"), and somewhat emotional norms ("a genuine and affecting manner").

Emotionality triumphs over the aesthetic in popular urban lyrics: "Marie does not sing that she is going steady with Pepíček and that she will be married within a year, but that blue-eyed Pepíček is chasing some other girl. Anna, while scrubbing the floor, does not complain that she would like to spend a pleasant afternoon in the park, but rather that she longs only for the dark grave. . . . Basically Marie is not a deeply melancholy creature; on the contrary, one would say that she is a gossip and a giggler. Well then, if Marie wishes to rise to higher spheres (which is ultimately the most serious goal of poetry and music) she will attain the region of sad and inconsolable feelings; nothing ennobles her so much as the prospect that she will soon be in her coffin wearing a wreath on her brow."[46] Emotional disturbances, not only as a direct reaction to reality, but also as a pure function of some thing (i.e. a song being performed), dominate in popular urban songs, and the emotional norm subordinates the aesthetic norm. The more touching the song, the more valuable it is. Concerning the difference between the hierarchy of norms in popular verse and in lofty poetry, a transformation typically occurs as soon as the form of the urban popular song penetrates into artistic poetry. Immediately its emotional norm,

[46] K. Čapek: *"Písně lidu pražského," Marsyas.*

through a transformation which we have already discussed, becomes an aesthetic norm.[47] The division between the superiority and subordination of the aesthetic
function thus corresponds to the social division between
the stratum which is the actual source of cultural activity
and the urban popular stratum.

We have treated the sociology of the aesthetic norm
in broad outline. It was shown that the approach to the
problem of the aesthetic norm through sociology is not
only a possible approach, or simply an ancillary one, but
is, together with the noetic aspect of the problem,
a basic requirement for research, since it enables us to
investigate in detail the dialectical contradiction between
the variability and multiplicity of the aesthetic norm and
its rights to constant validity. We noted further that the
aesthetic norm, having its source in the art of that social
stratum which is the bearer of cultural activity, is constantly renewing itself. Older norms as a rule descend
the ladder of the social hierarchy. Often, however, having sunk as low as they possibly can, they suddenly re-
appear in the art of the culturally leading stratum. This
is, of course, only a general outline of a process whose
actual development is complicated by the influence of
horizontal social divisions and by variations in the ties
between the aesthetic norm and other norms, the latter
involving the strength of the mutual bonds of various
types of norms and their hierarchical distribution. Both
the general outline and, even more, its complexities
testify that the aesthetic norm cannot be understood as
an *a priori* law which, with the accuracy of a measuring
instrument, would indicate the optimal conditions for
aesthetic pleasure. It is, rather, living energy which, with
all the variety of its manifestations—and even because of

---

[47]Cf. the article on Vítěslav Hálek in *Slovo a slovesnost,* I, 1935.

them—organizes the area of aesthetic phenomena and
provides a direction to its development. On the other
hand, even if the possibility of a general and *a priori*
valid aesthetic norm turns out to be illusory—since the
fundamental, anthropologically based principles of rhythm, symmetry, etc., despite their importance for the
noetics of the aesthetic norm, are not ideal aesthetic
norms—it was shown that the aesthetic norm does indeed
exist and operate. Acknowledging its changeability does
not invalidate its importance nor deny its very existence.

## III

Having discussed the aesthetic function and norm,
we now turn to aesthetic value. At first glance it might
seem that the problem of aesthetic value has been ex-
hausted by discussion of the aesthetic function (the force
which creates value), and of the aesthetic norm (the rule
by which it is measured). But we have shown in the two
preceding chapters: 1. The area of the aesthetic function
is broader than that of aesthetic value in the strict sense
of the word, since in cases where the aesthetic function
merely accompanies another function, the question of
aesthetic value is also only secondary in judging a given
item or action. 2. Fulfillment of the norm is not a necessary condition of aesthetic value, especially when that
value dominates others, that is, in art. From this it follows that art is the proper domain of aesthetic value,
being the privileged locus of aesthetic phenomena. While
value is subject to a norm outside art, here the norm is subject to value. Outside art, fulfillment of the norm is synonymous with value. In art the norm is often violated and
only sometimes fulfilled, and even then fulfillment is a

means, not an end. Fulfilling the norm causes aesthetic pleasure; aesthetic value may, however, include, in addition to pleasure, strong elements of displeasure, remaining all the time an undivided whole.[48] Application of the aesthetic norm subjects an individual case to a general rule and concerns a single aspect, its aesthetic function, which need not be dominant. Aesthetic evaluation, on the contrary, treats a phenomenon in all its complexity, since all extra-aesthetic functions and values are important as components of aesthetic value:[49] for this same reason aesthetic evaluation considers a work of art as a closed whole (unit) and is an individualizing act; aesthetic value in art is unique and cannot be repeated.

The problem of aesthetic value must thus be examined by itself. Its basic problem concerns the validity and range of aesthetic evaluation. Starting from this point, we have equally open paths in two directions: an examination of the variability of the concrete act of evaluation, and a search for the noetic premises of the objective (i.e., independent of the perceiver) validity of aesthetic judgment.

Let us first consider the variability of modern aesthetic evaluation. Immediately we are immersed in the sociology of art. First of all, the work of art itself is not a constant. Every shift in time, space or social surroundings alters the existing artistic tradition through whose prism the art work is observed, and as a result of such shifts that aesthetic object also changes which in the awareness of a member of a particular collective

[48]Cf. F. W. J. von Schelling: *Schriften zur Philosophie der Kunst*, Leipzig, 1911, p. 7: *"In dem wahren Kunstwerk gibt es keine einzelne Schönheit, nur das Ganze ist schön."*
[49]Cf. my article: *"Básnické dílo jako soubor hodnot. Jízdní řád literatury a poezie," Studie z estetiky*, Prague, 1966, pp. 140-43.

corresponds to a material artifact—an artistic product. And even, for example, when a certain work in two chronologically separate periods is evaluated affirmatively and equally, the aesthetic object being evaluated is a different one in each case, and hence, in some sense, is a different work. It is natural that with these shifts of the aesthetic object, aesthetic value also changes rather frequently. We often find, in the history of art, that a certain work shifts from a positive to a negative value over a period of time, or that it changes from a lofty, outstanding value to one which is mediocre, and vice versa. There is often a pattern of a rapid rise followed by a drop and then a second rise, but up to a different level of aesthetic value.[50] Conversely, some works of art remain for long periods of time on a high level with no decline: these are "eternal" values such as, in poetry, the works of Homer, at least since the Renaissance, in drama, the works of Shakespeare or Molière, in painting the works of Raphael or Rubens. And even though every age perceives these works differently—a tangible example is the evolution in the visual aspects of the plays of Shakespeare—nevertheless the works will always, or nearly always, be ranked at the top of the scale of aesthetic values. It would be erroneous to see this as indicating a lack of change. In the first place it is probable that if we look more closely, we will discover, even among the above works, fluctuations—often quite considerable—and, secondly, the concept of "highest aesthetic value" is not unambiguous. It depends on whether a work is seen as a "living" value or one which is "historical," "representative" or "academic," "exclusive" or "popular," etc. In all these nuances, alternating one with

[50]Cf. the monograph on Polák, *"Vznešenost přírody,"* Sborník filologický, Českd akademie věd, Prague, 1934.

the other, sometimes implementing several at once, a work of art can remain continually among the "eternal" values, and this persistence will not be a state, but— just as with works which change their positions in the scale—a process.

Thus aesthetic value is changeable at all levels, and passive inertia is impossible; "eternal" values vary and interchange, however, now more slowly, now less detectably than do less lofty values. But even the very ideal of unaltered duration of aesthetic value, independently of external influences, is not at all times or under all circumstances the highest or only desirable possibility. Finally, coexisting with art which has been created for the greatest duration and validity, we find art which is intentionally created for temporary validity, for "consumption." This category includes "private" or cryptic poetry created by an artist for a narrow circle of friends, nonce works which are thematically dependent on knowledge of circumstances existing for a short period or are known only to a limited circle of people. In visual art the claim to a lasting form of artistic value is often expressed in the choice of materials. Wax sculpture, for example, apparently results from a different anticipated duration than marble or bronze sculpture. Mosaic, too, has a different implicit life and value expectancy than does, e.g., water color, etc. Thus "consumer" art continually contrasts with "lasting" art. There are times when artists prefer an intensive, brief appeal rather than a gradually increasing, more lasting appeal. Today's art provides a good example. The Symbolist period recently sought values which were as durable as possible and were not dependent on changes in taste and incidental audiences. Mallarmé foundered in striving for the "absolute' work. In Czech literature Březina exemplifies the occasional conviction that it is possible to find "the supreme (i.e. metrical) form so polished that nothing more perfect would be possible."[51] Compare the above with the statement of a contemporary artist, André Breton:[52]

> "Picasso is, to me, great only because he has constantly remained in a defensive position with respect to objects in the external world, including those which he himself made. He never considered his works as anything more than mere *moments* of contact between himself and the world. Fleeting and ephemeral qualities, in contrast to what is usually the joy and pride of artists, were, to him, desirable in themselves. During the twenty years which have passed since his work was created the newspaper fragments pasted into his pictures have yellowed, their ink, formerly fresh, contributed a great deal to the arrogance of those magnificent "papiers collés" from 1913. The sunlight has bleached and the dampness has, in places, viciously wrinkled the magnificent blue and pink clippings. And this is good. The astonishing guitars pasted together from shabby laths, truly bridges of chance constantly in the process of rebuilding, day after day, across the stream of song, have not withstood the frantic stampede of singers. But everything happened as if Picasso had anticipated this impoverishment, this weakening, even disintegration. It seems as though he wished in advance to enter a conflict whose result has been indubitable, but which is fought by the creations of human hands against the natural elements, in order that he, through a

---

[51] Cf. my preface to the Hartl edition of *Žalmy* by Hlaváček, Prague, 1934, p. 12.
[52] *Point du jour*, Paris, p. 200.

compromise, could achieve what was most valuable, i.e. most real, during the very process of decay."

The changeability of aesthetic value is thus not a mere secondary phenomenon resulting from an "imperfection" in artistic creativity or perception, i.e. from human inability to attain an ideal, but belongs to the very basis of aesthetic value, which is a process and not a state, *energeia* and not *ergon*. Thus even without a change in time and space aesthetic value appears as a varied and complex activity which is expressed in the divergent opinions of critics about newly created.works of art, the inconstancy of consumer demand in the book and art markets, etc. Here, too, the present period provides a good illustration, with its rapid changes in preferences for art works. We need only observe the very quick price changes of literary works in the book market, the rapid rise and fall of prices in the area of the visual arts, etc. This is just a speeded-up film of a process which is operative in all periods of history. The causes of this value dynamics are, as indicated by Karel Teige,[53] social in nature: relaxation of the relationship between the consumer and the artist, between society and art. In previous eras, too, the process of aesthetic evaluation always reacted quickly to the dynamics of social interactions, since it was contemporaneous with and predetermined by such interactions and, in reacting, affected them in turn.

Society creates the institutions and organs with which it influences aesthetic value through regulation or evaluation of art works. Among these institutions are criticism, expertise, artistic training (including art schools

[53] *Jarmark umění,* Prague, 1936.

and institutions whose goal is the cultivation of passive contemplation), the marketing of art works and its advertizing, surveys to determine the most valuable work of art, art shows, museums, public libraries, competitions, prizes, academies, and, frequently, censorship. Each of these institutions has its own specific aims and may have a purpose other than simply to influence the status and development of aesthetic evaluation (e.g. a museum's goal is to assemble material for scientific research, etc.) and these other aims can often be primary ones (e.g. in censorship, the regimentation of extra-aesthetic functions of a work in the interests of the state and the ruling social and moral order). Nevertheless, all the goals share in influencing aesthetic value, and are at the same time models of certain social tendencies. Thus, for example, critical assessment is often interpreted as a search for objective aesthetic values, at other times as a manifestation of a special relationship of the judge to the work being judged or, again, as the popularization of new art works which are difficult for laymen to comprehend, or, finally, as propaganda for a certain tendency in art. They are all elements of every critical act, and in any particular case some always predominate, but above all the critic is always either the spokesman or conversely the antagonist or even a dissident from some social formation (class, environment, etc.). Arne Novák accurately pointed out in his lecture on the history of Czech criticism (delivered to the Prague Linguistic Circle in April, 1936) that, for example, the negative criticism by Chmelenský of Mácha's *Máj* is not only a display of a chance personal dislike by a critic of Mácha, but equally and most importantly—in the context of the other critical activity of Chmelenský and his theoretical views on the task of criticism—as an attempt by a narrow literary environment of that time to halt the influx of unfamiliar aesthetic values which would erode the taste and ideology of that environment. It is significant that at that same time or shortly afterwards the reading public did expand with respect to social origins, as Arne Novák also demonstrated in the same lecture.

The process of aesthetic evaluation is thus connected with the development of society, and an investigation of this process would form a chapter in the sociology of art. We should not, of course, forget the fact, introduced in the preceding chapter, that in a given society there is not just one level of poetic art, visual art, etc., but there are always several levels (*avant garde*, official, tabloid, urban folk, etc.), and consequently several degrees of aesthetic value. Each of these types lives its own life, but sometimes the various types meet and affect one another. A value which has lost its effectiveness in one may, by sinking or rising, enter another. Since this stratification corresponds, though not always directly or exactly, to the stratification of society, the multi-leveled nature of art contributes to the complicated process of creating and transforming aesthetic values.

We should add that the collective nature and character of aesthetic evaluation is also reflected in individual aesthetic judgments. The evidence for this is abundant. Publishers' questionnaires have shown, for example, that readers most frequently decide to purchase books not because of the opinions of professional critics—which seem to them to be too much colored by the individual tastes of the critics—but on the basis of statements by friends who are members of the same reading public as the buyers.[54] The authority of annual reader surveys

---

[54] Viz. L. Schücking: *Die Soziologie der literarischen Geschmacksbildung,* Leipzig and Berlin, 1931, p. 51.

is also well known. Collectors of visual art often choose a work simply because the name of the artist who created it is a label of generally recognized value. This explains why art dealers strive to create such a name-value[55] and discloses the importance of experts whose job it is to attribute or confirm authorship of art works.[56]

Aesthetic value turns out to be a process whose movement is influenced both by the immanent development of the artistic structure itself (cf. the current tradition against which every work is evaluated) and by the motion and shifts in the structure of social life. The position of a work of art on a certain level of aesthetic value, the duration of its stay on that level, any change in position, or finally the complete removal from the scale of aesthetic values—all depend not only on the properties of the actual material work but on other factors as well. Only the work itself endures, passing from one time period into another, or from one place to another, one social milieu to another. We cannot at this point discuss relativity, since for the evaluator, situated in a specific time and place, and in a given social milieu, any particular value of some work appears to him as necessary and constant.

Does this satisfactorily resolve—or simply avoid— the question of the objectivity of aesthetic value inherent in the material manifestation of a work of art? Does this question—which has been treated for centuries, sometimes metaphysically, sometimes by appeals to the anthropological make-up of man, sometimes, finally, by the concept of the art work as a unique and therefore definitive term—does this question lose all validity and urgency? There are, despite our acknowledgement of the

[55] K. Teige: *Jarmark umění*, p. 28n.
[56] M. J. Friedländer: *Der Kunstkenner*, Berlin, 1920.

changeability of aesthetic evaluation, some phenomena which testify that it has not lost its importance. How do we explain, for example, the fact that among works of the same movement, even of the same artist and hence among works arising from roughly identical strata of artistic structure and social origin, some works are not valued highly, while others are valued most highly with a persistence which borders on self-evidence? It is also obvious that there is not such a great gulf between enthusiastically affirmative and intensely negative evaluation as there is between both of these types of evaluation and complete indifference. Finally, it frequently happens that praise and damnation are encountered simultaneously in the criticism of a single work. Is this not another indication that focusing attention—be it acceptance or rejection—on a given work may be based, at least in some cases, on an objectively higher aesthetic valuation of the work? Additionally, how are we to grasp—if not through the hypothesis of an objective aesthetic value—the fact that a given work of art may be recognized as a positive aesthetic value even by those critics who, in other respects, relate to it very negatively, as happened in the reception of Mácha's *Máj* by Czech criticism of the period? The history of art, even when its methodology attempts to reduce as much as possible the role of evaluation to historically propounded value,[57] must, nevertheless, constantly deal with the problem of aesthetic value which is inherent in a given work regardless of its historical aspects. One can even say that the existence of this problem testifies to the constantly recurring attempts to restrict its influence to historical investigation. Finally, let us recall that every struggle for a new aesthetic value in art, just as every counterattack against it, is organized

[57]Cf. my monograph on Polák's *Vznešenost přírody*, p. 6n.

in the name of an objective and lasting value. Only by assuming an objective aesthetic value can we, after all, explain the fact that "a truly great artist cannot conceive
of life being shown, or beauty fashioned, under any conditions other than those that he has selected."[58]

Thus in the work of art which is not subject to external influences it is impossible to avoid the problem of
objective aesthetic value. It is, however, necessary to pre-
pare for its resolution by carefully analyzing the concept
"objective aesthetic value." For us there can be no doubt
that art created by man for man cannot create value
which is independent of man (as far as the appearances
of the aesthetic function outside of art are concerned,
we showed in the preceding chapter that even here there
can be no question of aesthetic efficacy as an enduring
property of an object). The solution chosen by, for example, scholastic philosophy[59] and which is echoed by
O. Wilde, consists in distinguishing between the unchanging ideal of beauty and its varying realizations. This solution may have the semblance of validity only as long
as it is derived from an entire system of metaphysics.
Otherwise it seems to be a forced solution with doubtful
value. If we do not wish to admit the inappropriate mixture of noetics and metaphysics we could think, as we
did with the aesthetic norm, about the anthropological
structure of man which is common to all men and valid
as a basic, unchanging connection between man and a
work, a tie which, if we project it to a material phenomenon, would appear as an objective aesthetic value.
But the problem is that a work of art as a whole (for
only a whole is an aesthetic value) is at bottom a *sign*, di-
rected to man as a member of an organized collective

[58]Oscar Wilde: "The Critic as Artist."
[59]Compare J. Maritain: *Art et scolastique,* Paris, 1927, p. 43n.

and not just to an anthropological constant. Oscar Wilde said, correctly, of art ("The Critic as Artist") that ". . . the meaning of any beautiful created thing is, at least, as much in the soul of him who looks at it as it was in his soul who wrought it. Nay, it is rather the beholder who lends to the beautiful thing its myriad meanings and makes it marvellous for us and sets it in some new relation to the age, so that it becomes a vital portion of our lives. . . ."

Even if we search among the noetic possibilities and hypotheses of *objective* aesthetic value it is impossible to escape the grasp of the social character of art. It is not a matter, of course, of examining the ties existing between a concrete work of art and a concrete collective, i.e., of the sociology of art, but rather of a certain generally valid regularity which characterizes the ties between a work of art as an aesthetic value in general and some collective (even some member of some collective). The result of an attempt which has been conducted in this manner can, naturally, be only a general framework which acquires, in every concrete case, different contents and thus does allow us to deduce special critical rules. It is, however, obvious that given variability of evaluation, each concrete substantiation of aesthetic judgement is valid only with respect to the ties between the work and *that* society or *that* social structure from whose viewpoint the judgement is pronounced. A universally valid aesthetic value can be, from a temporally and socially limited viewpoint, only instinctively felt, and only through confrontation of judgements from many periods and environments indirectly ascertained. Much more important than the rule is the basic question: is objective aesthetic value a reality or a false illusion?

In an attempt to answer this question we advance the semiological aspect of art which was discussed above.

First of all, we ought to make a brief mention of the nature of the sign in general. A short definition would be: something which stands in place of something else and points to that other thing. For what purpose is the sign used? Most typically its function is to promote understanding among individuals as members of a single collective. This is the aim of language, the most highly developed and complete system of signs. But one must point out that the sign may have other functions in addition to the communicative function. Thus, for example, money is a sign replacing another reality in the function of economic values. Its goal is not communication, however, but facilitation of the flow of goods. The realm of communicative signs is therefore immeasurably broad. Any sort of fact may become a communicative sign. And art belongs in this area, though in a manner which distinguishes it from any other communicative sign.

In order to ascertain that specific difference which characterizes art as a sign, let us first turn our attention to that type of art in which the communicative function is found most clearly, for it is just this function which makes comparison possible. We are speaking of poetry and painting. As a rule literary and visual works contain some communication. Even if in some stages of their development the communicative function is weakened to a zero degree (e.g., absolute painting, suprematism, poetry in an artificial language), this weakening appears as a *negation* of the normal state and not as a normal state. In much the same way modern linguistics speaks of a "zero" ending—and not about the absence of some ending—in cases where the grammatical form is, by the lack of an ending, opposed to forms which have an ending. The ending belongs to the very *concept* of grammatical form, and communication, i.e. theme (content) belongs to the very concept of painting and poetry. Painting and literature are thematic arts. But is information which is contained in a work of literature or a painting actual information, or does it somehow differ from it? And how? It is different, precisely because the aesthetic function, by dominating over the informational function, has changed the very nature of the information.

An epic poem, as a purely communicative phenomenon, will tell about an event which happened in such and such places, at such and such times, and in such and such circumstances, and with such and such persons involved. But here is the difference: when we perceive a certain phenomenon as a communication we will be interested in the relation of the communication to the reality which it discusses. This means, whether it is specifically stated or not, that the reception of the phenomenon from the point of view of the receiver will be accompanied by the question of whether that which the speaker is saying actually happened, whether the details of those events were such as he describes. This does not mean that an answer to this question must be affirmative. The answer may very well indicate that the phenomenon was partly or entirely fictitious. The listener will guess at, or ask for confirmation of, the intention of the speaker. And from this investigation, or simple guesswork, there arises a further modification of the material relation of the phenomenon (i.e. its relation to reality). For example: yes, we are dealing with a fictional phenomenon intended to deceive the listener, to direct his behavior away from the correct path, thus we are dealing with a lie; or: we have here a fictional phenomenon intended to present an unreal event as a real one with no intention of altering the behavior of the listener, but simply with the aim of testing the listener's credulity. Hence it is merely a case of mystification. Or yet again:

we have a fictional phenomenon with no intent to deceive the listener, but simply aimed at offering him the possibility of some other reality than the one he is living in, to comfort or alarm him by the difference between the invented reality and the real one . . . hence a case of pure fiction.

But in a case where we consider a narrative linguistic phenomenon as a literary product with a dominant aesthetic function, the relation to the phenomenon will suddenly be different and the entire structure of the material ties of the phenomenon will present a different aspect. The question of whether a narrated story did or did not happen will lose for the listener (reader) its vital significance, and there will be no mention of whether the author wished to, or was able to, deceive. We are not asserting that the question of the real basis of the narrated event ceased to exist. The fact of whether, to what degree and in what manner the writer presents the narrated event as real or fictitious, will be, on the contrary, an important element of the structure of the literary work. Nuances within this *manner* of presentation are often the bases which differentiate techniques in various artistic movements (Romanticism, some aspects of Realism) and genres (story, fairy tale), as well as the mutual relationship of individual elements and parts within a given work. Thus in the historical novel we often find a differentiation between the characters and events in the foreground, which are fictional, and those in the background, which are real. The question of the real basis of a narrated event, if we consider it from the standpoint of the structure of a work and the manner of presentation, is fundamentally different from the question of the real *communicative* content of the narrated event, which, for example, a literary historian would ask of a work. The historian, in dealing with *Babička* by B.

Němcová, may ask whether the young authoress actually experienced the events in her story, whether the Pankl family actually lived in Staré bělidlo, etc. For the reader, the question of truthfulness will be: did the authoress at all, or to what degree, wish that her work be understood as a documentary narration of the history of her childhood? The (possibly unstated) answer to this question, (even if the question was not completely formulated) will determine the entire emotional and conceptual atmosphere which envelops this work by Němcová for this reader; it will determine the semantic nuances of the whole and of the details. "Fictionality" in literature is thus something totally different from communicative fiction. All modifications of the material ties of linguistic phenomena which appear in communicative speech can also play a role in literature, and falsehood is one example. But here it acts as an element of structure and not of real-life values having practical importance. Baron Munchausen, if he had really lived, would be a swindler, and his speech would be nothing but lies. But the writer who invented Munchausen and his lies is not a liar but simply a writer, and the statements by Munchausen are, in his presentation, poetic acts.

Well then, given this state of affairs, does the artistic sign lack any direct and necessary contact with reality? Is art in relation to reality less than a shadow which at least tells of the presence of an object, even if the viewer can not see it? One can find, in the history of art, movements which would have answered affirmatively the question just posed. Thus, for example, the aesthetic theory of K. Lange, who interprets art as illusion, or the theory of F. Paulhan, who said that art is founded on a lie. All theories tending to hedonistic and aesthetic subjectivism are close to this position (art as a stimulus to pleasure, art as the sovereign creation of a hitherto nonexistent reality).

But these views still do not reveal the true essence of art. In order to explain their error, let us start from a concrete example. Imagine a reader of Dostoevsky's *Crime and Punishment*. The question of whether the story about the student, Raskolnikov, actually happened is, in addition to what we have already stated, outside the pale of the reader's interests. Nevertheless the reader feels the strong relationship of the novel to reality: not to that reality which is described in the novel — to events set in Russia in a certain year of the nineteenth century — but to the reality which the reader himself is familiar with, to situations which he has experienced, or, given the circumstances in which he lives, he might experience, to feelings and unrestrained emotions which might — or actually did — accompany the situations, to actions on the part of the reader which might have been caused by the situations. About the novel which has absorbed the reader there have accumulated not one but many realities. The deeper the work has absorbed the reader, the greater is the area of current and vitally important realities of the reader to which the work attaches a material relationship. The change which the material relationship of the work — the sign — has undergone is thus simultaneously its weakening and strengthening. It is weakened in the sense that the work does not refer to the reality which it directly depicts, and strengthened in that the work of art as a sign acquires an indirect (figurative) tie with realities which are vitally important to the perceiver, and through them to the entire universe of the perceiver as a collection of values. Thus the work of art acquires the ability to refer to a reality which is totally different from the one which it depicts, and to systems of values other than the one from which it arose and on which it is founded.

At this point in our discussion we have the

opportunity to direct our attention to art forms other
than those which have "content," to athematic art such
as music and architecture, in order to determine whether
they too can acquire that complex material connection
which differentiates products of thematic arts from gen-
uinely informational phenomena. Music, by its very
nature is not referential. Through the use of devices
such as quotations, author's quotations,[60] it may tend
toward referential function, but this tendency is a negation of the very nature of music. In poetry and painting,
negation plays an opposite role, that is, they gravitate
toward athematics. Although a musical phenomenon is
not referential, it can very intensively involve the
complex material tie to diverse regions of the life experience of the perceiver, and thus to values which are valid
for him, values which we have discussed in thematic arts
as being characteristic of phenomena with a dominant
aesthetic function. Oscar Wilde, in the essay cited above,
has accurately described this complex and, despite its
objective vagueness, intensive material relationship of
music:

> "After playing Chopin, I feel as if I had been weep-
> ing over sins that I had never committed, and
> mourning over tragedies that were not my own.
> Music always seems to me to produce that effect.
> It creates for one a past of which one has been
> ignorant, and fills one with a sense of sorrows that
> have been hidden from one's tears. I can fancy a
> man who has led a perfectly commonplace life,
> hearing by chance some curious piece of music, and
> suddenly discovering that his soul, without his
> being conscious of it, had passed through terrible

[60]Cf. O. Zich: *Estetika dramatického umění*, Prague, 1931, p. 277n.

experiences, and known fearful joys, or wild romantic loves, or great renunciations."

Experiences which a man has not had, but could
have had, a potential biography without concrete content—this is how Wilde describes the material ties of
music. His words are a poetic expression for the multiplicity and the implicit referential vagueness of the material relationship of the art work as sign. For the same
reason another poet, Paul Valéry, calls the emotions
aroused by music "inexhaustible."[61] That music which
completely lacks an informational function, reveals more
clearly than thematic art the specific nature of the artistic sign. What is the carrier of meaning in this case? Not
content, which does not exist here, but formal components: tonal level, melodic and rhythmic structure,
etc. For this reason the material connection serves much
more to provide a certain overall approach to reality
than would be the case with the revelation of some individual reality. But this is simply a general property of art
as sign, only here it is more obviously disclosed.

The case of architecture is close to that of music, as
P. Valéry noted in his dialogue-essay *Eupalinos;* Socrates

[61]*Eupalinos.* Elsewhere in this work he treats the impression aroused
in him while listening to music: "Was it not a changeable richness, analo-
gous to a constant flame, illuminating and warming its entire being throughout the continual burning of memories, forebodings, langours and predic-
tions, and through an infinite number of emotional agitations having no
specific motivation." Cf. also H. Delacroix: *Psychologie de l'art,* Paris,
1937, p. 210n. The world of music is autonomous and does not wish to depend on the world of ordinary acoustical phenomena. But nevertheless it
has the (semantic) potential belonging to language and non-musical sounds.
Music generalizes feelings by descending to the rhythmical waves of absolute emotion. Thus there arises a musical form whose structure outlines the
emotional agitation occurring at deeper levels of the emotional life than
ordinary emotional disturbances. This internal dynamism, of which music
is an outline, is transformed by contact with it, and through it, and becomes its own symbol and expression.

speaks, in the essay, of music and architecture: "The art of which we are speaking must, in contrast to the other arts, engender in us, using numbers and numerical relationships, not only a theme, but also that hidden power which gives rise to all themes." But a distinction must be made, because architecture, in addition to what Valéry stated, also "speaks," i.e. it imparts information, even if of a totally different type from information in literature or painting. Information contained in an architectonic work is closely connected with the practical function which the work implements. A building "means" its purpose, i.e. the acts and processes which are to be carried out within its confines (delimited and formed by its materials): "Here," says the building, "merchants gather. Here judges judge. Here prisoners lament. Here lovers revel. These business shops, courts and prisons speak eloquently whenever those who built them understood their purpose."[62] Information contained in an architectonic work is, however, usually totally overshadowed and concealed by the practical function with which it is closely connected. It becomes visible only when the building pretends to a function other than the one it actually fulfills: an apartment building in the form of a palace, a factory which looks like a castle, etc. The assuming of an identity (palace, castle) becomes an actual communication to the perceiver.[63] But because of all the remaining instances in

[62] P. Valéry: *Eupalinos*.

[63] We should note in this connection, if only briefly, that one of the themes in architecture is the symbolic effect of a work of architecture. The effect is particularly noticeable in those stages of development when a building, especially a public building, represents the ideology of the milieu from which it arose and which it serves, or when it represents its power and social importance. Note, for example, the symbolic effect of the medieval castles and cathedrals, or the palatial buildings of the Renaissance and Baroque.

which the original intent is concealed by the actual one, communication is almost impossible, and the dominant activity is left to an indefinite and variable material bond which is specific for the art work. Here, too, this bond is borne and determined by "formal" plastic means. The process of forming the varied material ties is graphically described by Valéry in the above-mentioned dialogue, where Phèdre relates an impression of an architectonic work:

> "No one ever noticed, standing in front of material which has been delicately deprived of weight and is, to all appearances, very simple, that his attention is directed to some vibration of happiness by almost imperceptible curves, nearly invisible but omnipotent roundings, and profound combinations of correctness and incorrectness which the artist simultaneously created and concealed, giving them such an irresistible quality that they became indefinable. They led the moving viewer, guided by their invisible presence, from vision to vision, from profound silence to a whisper of delight as he approached or retreated, again approached and wandered about within sight of the work, being directed only by the work and becoming the plaything of his own wonderment. 'I wish,' said the man from Mégare (i.e. the master builder Eupalinos), 'that my temple would affect a person in the same way that he is affected by his beloved.' "

"Athematic" art has thus shown that a specific material tie joining a work of art as sign with reality is conveyed not only by the content, but also by all other components. Let us now digress again to thematic arts in order to discover whether their "formal components" can become, or already are, always semantic factors and bearers of the material connection as well. Let us look at painting, since, concerning poetry it is—thanks to functional linguistics—clear today that all of its elements, in their capacity as parts of a linguistic system, are bearers of semantic energy, from sound groups to sentence structure. In painting the situation is different. There, it may seem at first glance that the material with which this art deals, i.e. a surface, color patches, lines . . . is a purely optical affair. More complex and secondary elements, perspective and color spaces, contours, are of course here, too, clearly semantic factors. The enumerated basic elements are not without the possibility of acquiring a material connection. Framed space is different from merely a field of vision, even if in some cases its contents may correspond totally to it. Limitation by the frame gives them certain semantic properties, above all whatever is contained within the frame has a semantic unity (whole). Lines divide the surface: the process of the viewer's attention is governed by their direction and course. They determine not only the optical but also the semantic organization of the framed segment. The lines take over the function of contours even when the picture aims at non-objectivity, although no object is depicted in such cases. "Objectless" objectivity arises as a pure concept. These semantic properties of the line were employed by several movements in modern painting such as absolute painting (Kandinsky) and those closely related to it. Even color patches are not only optical phenomena but semantic as well. The very quality of color has far-reaching semantic possibilities. The symbolics of colors is a well-known cultural-historical fact. In the Middle Ages its use was widespread and well-established.[64] It is natural that color symbolism also

[64]Cf. for example, Zibrt: *"Symbolika barev u starých Čechů," Listy z českých dějin kulturnich,* Prague, 1891.

affected painting. "Why does Christ always wear a blue garment? Because the eyes of the faithful were always turned yearningly to the sky, the home of the heavenly bridegroom and the abode of the faithful after death."[65] Thus blue became the noblest color of the Christians, even though its psychological effect places it among the "cold" colors. Even today, when color symbolism does not comprise a rigid system and does not stand in the center of interest, and, even in non-objective painting, where the meaning of color cannot be attached to a depicted object, one can note a semantic quality of color; thus, for example, the color blue, especially if it occupies continuously the upper part of a depicted area, will, even in a work with no object depiction, evoke the meaning of "sky"; where it occupies the lower part of the space, it will be interpreted as "water." The relation of color to space also involves color quality. The well known fact that "warm" colors appear to move forward and "cool" colors backward, has not only optical content but also semantic. Thus, for example, it is possible in non-objective painting to create a space without material effect, simply space-meaning, purely through the use of a combination of the two abovementioned color groups. Further, color areas are the bearers of contours, just as lines are. Contours evoke the meaning of objectness, however, even if no particular object is evoked. For this reason Suprematist painting, which of all movements in painting went furthest in the tendency to suppression of any "content," preferred as the shape of color groups either the square or the rectangle, the most indifferent geometric forms, in order that the color patch might cease to influence by means of its form,

---

[65]T. Wohlbehr: *Bau und Leben der bildenden Kunst,* Leipzig and Berlin, 1914.

and would (as far as it was possible) become a purely optical value without semantic shadings of object-ness. In modern painting the contour meaning of color areas is sometimes revealed by having the outline of the important color area partly covered and partly divergent from linear contours. One could enumerate other semantic effects of colors. The difference between color as a characteristic of an object (localized color), for example, and color as light—such a difference has a semantic quality.

Thus the formal elements of painting are semantic factors just as linguistic elements are in literature. But of themselves they are not tied by any material connection to a certain object but, like elements in a musical work, they bear potential semantic energy which, emanating from the total work, indicates a certain attitude toward the world of reality.

We have analyzed the sign (semantic) character of the work of art. It was shown that art is closely related to the area of informational signs, but in such a way that it is a dialectical negation of actual information. Genuine information refers to an actual concrete reality known to the one who gives the sign, and about which the one to whom the sign is given can be informed. In art, however, the reality about which the work directly provides information (in thematic art) is not the real source of the material connection, but only its intermediary. The real tie in this situation is a variable one, and points to realities known to the viewer. They are not and can in no way be expressed or even indicated in the work itself, because it forms a component of the viewer's intimate experience. This cluster of realities may be very important and the material tie of the art work with each of them is indirect, figurative. The realities with which the art work can be confronted in the consciousness and subconsciousness of the viewer are squeezed into the general, intellectual, emotional and wilful attitude which the viewer assumes toward reality in general. The experience which surges through the viewer as a result of confronting the work of art spreads to the total image of reality in the viewer's thoughts. The indefinite nature of the material tie of the work of art is compensated by the fact that it is paralleled by the perceiving individual who reacts, not partially but with all aspects of his attitude toward the world and reality. The question now arises: is the interpretation of the art work, as sign, only an individual property which differs from one person to the next and which cannot be compared? The answer to this question was anticipated earlier in our statement that the work is a *sign,* and hence at bottom is a social fact. Also, the attitude which the individual takes toward reality is not the exclusive property even of the strongest personalities, for it is to a considerable extent, and in weaker persons almost totally, determined by the social relationships in which the individual is involved. Thus the result arrived at by the analysis of the sign-like nature of the art work in no way leads to aesthetic subjectivism: we merely concluded that the material ties entered into by the work as sign set in motion the attitude of a viewer toward reality. But the viewer is a social creature, a member of a collective. This affirmation leads us a step closer to our goal; if the material connection introduced by the work affects the manner in which the individual and the collective address themselves to reality, it becomes evident that one important task for us is to treat the question of extra-aesthetic values contained in a work of art.

The work of art, even when it does not overtly or indirectly contain evaluations, is saturated with values. Everything in it, from the medium—even the most material medium (e.g., stone or bronze as used in sculpture)—to the most thematic formations, contains values. Evaluation, as we have seen, lies at the very basis of the specific nature of the artistic sign. The material bond of the work involves, by virtue of its multiplicity, not only individual objects but reality as a whole, and thus affects the total attitude of the viewer to reality. It is he who is the source and regulator of evaluation. Since every element of the art work, be it "content" or "form," acquires that complex material bond in the context of the work, each element acquires extra-aesthetic values.

Values held by individual elements of one and the same work enter into mutual relationships, sometimes positive, sometimes negative. Thus they mutually influence one another, and it can happen that a given material element could, depending on the circumstances, possess totally opposite values:

> "Atomism in treating the form of a work of art occurs when the investigator divides the form into components (i.e. straight and curved lines, convex and concave lines, visibly defined and indistinct, etc.) and assigns a constant meaning to each element (e.g., bright colors indicate optimism, dark colors imply pessimism, straight lines stand for clarity and brevity, immediacy and accuracy, reasonableness and purposefulness). Criticism of this approach should stress the fact that formal elements can be completely grasped only in relation to the whole, and, their meaning varies considerably depending on their distribution within that whole. Thus, for example, black between bright colors may have a solemn and stately effect, as it does in portraits by Rubens; a straight line may change its meaning from an almost mystical

experience of the absolute limitations caused by
one's own nature, to a rationalistic and mechanistic
statement. Equations such as comparing dark colors
to pessimism are too crude to use in expressing the
complicated inner life of a work of art."[66]

Extra-aesthetic values found in a work of art thus form
a unity, but it is a dynamic unity and cannot be established mechanically. The dynamic nature of a group of
extra-aesthetic values of a work may be so intense that,
within a work, there may be found a complete contradiction between two evaluations, e.g., degrading and ad-
miringly positive. Cf. the monumentalizing tradition of
"low" themes which is common in realistic painting of
the nineteenth century (*The Stonebreakers* by Courbet);
or the use of artistic devices from the heroic epos to
treat heroes and actions in literary genres which had
hitherto been assigned "low" classification. This approach was employed in the epic poetry of Romantic
poets.[67] Mutual conflict of extra-aesthetic values in a
work can be of the most varied kinds and intensities. But
even in cases where a maximum of quantity or intensity
is attained, the unity of the work is not destroyed. This
is because the unity does not appear as a mechanical ag-
gregation but is presented to the viewer as a challenge
which can be met by overcoming the contradictions encountered during the complex process of perceiving and
evaluating the work.

Extra-aesthetic values in art are thus not only properties of the work itself but also of the perceiver. The
latter, of course, approaches the work with his own

---

[66]H. Lützeler: *Einführung in die Philosophie der Kunst,* Bonn,
1934, p. 27.
[67]Cf. Ju. Tynjanov: *Arxaisty i novatory,* Leningrad, 1929.

system of values, with his own attitude toward reality. It frequently happens that a part, often a significant part, of the values which the perceiver obtains from the work is in conflict with the system which he himself holds. The manner in which such a conflict and its resulting tensions can arise is clear. The artist who created the work was from the same social milieu and the same period as the perceiver. In this case the conflicts between the values of the work of art and the perceiver result from a shift in artistic structure intended by the artist. Or the work stems from a different social and temporal milieu than the viewer—and conflicts in extra-aesthetic values are then inevitable.[68] So the art work as a collection of

[68] One might ask whether we should not consider cases of total agreement or, conversely, absolute disagreement in extra-aesthetic values between those contained in a work and those held by a viewer. Cases may arise in which total agreement, or at least a tendency toward it, occur. For example, in those art forms—usually "low"—which result from an attempt to make it very easy for the viewer to approach the work and to remove all obstacles from his path. Here, too, we have only a *tendency* which is never completely fulfilled, since a certain amount and a certain manner of disagreement between the evaluation of the perceiver and the values in the work will be present even in this situation. Cf., for example, the well-known fact that readers of romantic novels prefer to read works which come from a different milieu and depict a way of life different from that of the readers. With respect to the opposite possibility, i.e. total disagreement between values in a work and the value system of the viewer, there are many tendencies toward this extreme in the history of art, and sometimes they are accompanied by provocative intentions (cf. the satanism of a certain kind of Symbolism, which provocatively proclaimed the inversion of an entire system of values; evil a positive value, good a negative value, etc.). An insuperable mutual alienation of values held by the viewer *versus* those contained in a work of art may bring about a situation in which the work loses all meaning for the viewer and is not even seen as a work of art. Note, for example, the total lack of comprehension exhibited by viewers observing works from a milieu with which they have no contact whatsoever: the reactions of the seventeenth and eighteenth centuries to medieval art, all *maudit* poets and, in general, artists who often remain completely unnoticed during their lives, and become known only when the possibility of a connection—at least partially positive—arises between their work and the value system which is contending for validity.

extra-aesthetic values is not a mere replica of a system of values valid and obligatory for a perceiving collective. For the same reason values inhering in a work are not felt to be as mandatory as practical values which are expressed—as far as they ever are expressed—by purely communicative phenomena. A clear case is offered, for example, by censorship, which distinguishes between views expressed as information and those resulting either directly from the art work or directly expressed in it. Only extreme rigorousness in this respect can lead to equating art with an informational phenomenon.

We have arrived at a point from which it is possible to survey the mutual relationship between aesthetic value and the other values contained in a work of art, and to explain the true nature of that relationship. Previously we confined ourselves to the assertion that aesthetic value dominates all other values in a work of art. This assertion follows with logical necessity from the basis of art—that privileged region of aesthetic phenomena—which is, due to the dominance of the aesthetic function and aesthetic value, distinct from the countless number of other phenomena in which the aesthetic function is facultative and subordinate to some other function. Environments such as medieval or folklore societies, which do not have a clear differentiation of functions, do not, of course, intuit the dominance of the aesthetic function in art. They have no concept of art in the sense in which we understand it today; cf. the medieval inclusion of visual arts into the category of material products in the widest sense of the term. If we assert that aesthetic function and value in a work of art dominate over other functions and values, we are not offering a postulate for a practical relation to art (in which, even today, for some individuals and collectives, some other function is dominant). We are simply drawing a theoretical conclusion from the position which art occupies in the entire realm of aesthetic phenomena, assuming that differentiation of functions has been accomplished.

Even these avowedly theoretical formulations have been criticized, due to a misunderstanding, as espousing "formalism" and art-for-art's-sake. The self-sufficiency of the work of art, an aspect of the dominant position of aesthetic function and value, is mistakenly confused with the Kantian "disinterestedness" of art. In order to correct this error it is necessary to look at the position and character of aesthetic value in art from within artistic structure. That is, we must proceed from extra-aesthetic values—distributed among individual elements of a work—toward aesthetic value which binds the work into a unity. In so doing we discover something which is unique and unexpected. We said earlier that all elements of a work of art, in form and content, possess extra-aesthetic values which, within the work, enter into mutual relationships. The work of art appears, in the final analysis, as an actual collection of extra-aesthetic values and nothing else. The material components of the artistic artifact, and the manner in which they are used as artistic means, assume the role of mere conductors of energies introduced by extra-aesthetic values. If we ask ourselves at this point what has happened to aesthetic value, it appears that it has dissolved into individual extra-aesthetic values, and is really nothing but a general term for the dynamic totality of their mutual interrelationships. The distinction between "form" and "content" as used in the investigation of an art work is thus incorrect. The formalism of the Russian school of aesthetic and literary theory was correct in maintaining that all elements of a work are, without distinction, components of form. It must be added that all components are equally the bearers of meaning and extra-aesthetic values, and thus components of content. The analysis of "form" must not be narrowed to a mere formal analysis. On the other hand, however, it must be made clear that only the *entire* construction of the work, and not just the part called "content," enters into an active relation with the system of life values which govern human affairs.

The dominance of aesthetic value above all other values, a distinguishing feature of art, is thus something other than a mere external superiority. The influence of aesthetic value is not that it swallows up and represses all remaining values, but that it releases every one of them from direct contact with a corresponding life-value. It brings an entire assembly of values contained in the work as a dynamic whole into contact with a total system of those values which form the motive power of the life practice of the perceiving collective. What is the nature and goal of this contact? Above all it must be borne in mind, as we have already demonstrated, that this contact is rarely idyllically tranquil. As a rule the values contained in the art work are somewhat different, both in their mutual relationships and in the quality of individual values, from the complex system of values which is valid for the collective. There thus arises a mutual tension, and herein lies the particular meaning and effect of art. The constant necessity for practical application of values determines the free movement of the totality of values governing the life practice of the collective. The displacement of individual members of the hierarchy (re-valuation of values) is very difficult here, and is accompanied by strong shocks to the entire life practice of the given collective (slowing of development, uncertainty of values, disintegration of the system, even revolutionary eruptions). On the other hand, values in the art work—of which each by itself is free of actual dependency, but whose totality has potential validity—can, without harm, regroup and transform themselves. They can experimentally crystallize into a new configuration and dissolve an old one, can adapt to the development of the social situation and to new creative facts of reality, or at least seek the possibility of such adaptation.

Viewed in this light, the autonomy of the art work and the dominance of the aesthetic function and value within it appear not as destroyers of all contact between the work and reality—natural and social—but as constant stimuli of such contact. Art is a vital agent of great importance, even in periods of development and forms which stress self-orientation in art plus dominance of aesthetic function and value. Sometimes it is during just such stages which combine development and self-orientation that art may exert considerable influence on the relation of man to reality.[69]

Now we can finally return to the question from which we started: Is it possible, in some manner or other, to demonstrate the objective validity of aesthetic value? We have already said that the direct object of everyday aesthetic evaluation is not a "material" artifact, but an "aesthetic object" which is its expression and correlate in the viewer's awareness. But nevertheless an objective (i.e. independent and lasting) aesthetic value must be sought, if it exists, in a material artifact which endures alone and unchanging, whereas the aesthetic object is changeable, being determined not only by the organization and properties of the material artifact, but equally by the corresponding stage of development of the nonmaterial artistic structure. An independent aesthetic

[69]Cf. the case of *Máj*, by Mácha, which is treated in the essay "Příspěvky *k dnešní problematice básnického zjevu Máchova,*" *Listy pro umění a kritiku,* IV.

value inherent in a material artistic artifact, if we assume that it exists, has only a potential character compared to that of the everyday value of an aesthetic object. A material artistic artifact, having a certain organization, can unite, in the minds of its viewers, an aesthetic object and actual, positive aesthetic value, regardless of the stage of development of the given artistic structure. Then we can formulate the question of the existence of an objective aesthetic value only in the sense of whether such a construction of a material artistic artifact is possible.

How does a material artifact participate in the rise of an aesthetic object? We have already seen that its properties, and even the meaning resulting from their arrangement (content of the work), enter into the aesthetic object as bearers of extra-aesthetic values which in turn lead to complex mutual relationships, both positive and negative (similarities and differences), giving rise to a dynamic whole which retains its unity through similarities and is simultaneously set in motion by differences.

We can therefore say that the degree of independent value of an artistic artifact will be greater to the degree that the bundle of extra-aesthetic values which it attracts is greater, and to the degree that it is able to intensify the dynamism of their mutual connection. Of course we are not including changes in the quality of these values from one period to another. Customarily, the feeling of unity evoked by a work is considered the main criterion of aesthetic value. But unity should not be understood as something static, as complete harmony, but as dynamic, as a problem with which the work confronts the viewer. In this connection it is helpful to recall a remark by V. Šklovskij: "A winding road, a road on which one's foot feels the stones, a road which returns—

that is the road of art."[70] If the task faced by the viewer
is too simple, that is, if in a given situation similarities
outweigh differences, the effect of the work is weakened
and it quickly fades away, since the work does not force
the viewer to remain or to return. Therefore a work having a weakly based dynamics rapidly becomes automatic.
If, conversely, discovering unity in the work is too difficult for the viewer, i.e. if the differences outnumber the
similarities too greatly, it may happen that the viewer
will not be able to comprehend the work as a deliberate
construct. The influence of differences which create too
many hindrances never endangers the lasting effect of a
work so much as does the lack of them. The feeling of
disorientation, of an inability to grasp the unifying intent of a work of art, is a common experience when we
first encounter a completely unfamiliar artistic product.
A third possibility, of course, is that both similarities
and differences, conditioned by the construction of the
material artistic artifact, are very strong, but that they
achieve a mutual equilibrium. This case is obviously optimal and most completely fulfills the postulate of aesthetic value.

   We should not forget, however, that in addition to
the internal arrangement of the art work, and closely
tied to it, there also exists a relationship between the
work as a collection of values and those values possessing
practical validity for the collective which perceives the
work. In the course of its existence a material artifact
comes into contact with many different collectives and
many mutually differing value systems. How, in this situation, is the postulate of its independent aesthetic value
expressed? It is clear that here, too, differences are as
significant as are similarities. A work intended to

[70]*O teorii prozy,* Moscow-Leningrad, 1925, p. 21.

coincide completely with recognized life-values is perceived as a fact which is neither aesthetic nor artistic, but simply pretty *(Kitsch)*. Only a tension between extra-aesthetic values of a work and life-values of a collective enable a work to affect the relation between man and reality, and to affect is the proper task of art. Therefore we may say that the independent aesthetic value of an artistic artifact is higher and more enduring to the extent that the work does not lend itself to literal interpretation from the standpoint of a generally accepted system of values of some period and some milieu. If we return to the inner composition of the artistic artifact, it is certainly not difficult to conclude that works having great internal contradictions offer—depending on the degree of divergence and the diversity in significance which results—a much less convenient basis for the mechanical application of an entire system of values with practical validity than do works without internal differences or with only weak differences. Here too, therefore, multiplicity, variety and complexity of the material artifact are potential aesthetic assets. Independent aesthetic value of an artistic artifact resides, therefore, to all intents and purposes, in the tension, the overcoming of which is the task of the viewer. But this is something entirely different from that harmoniousness which is often suggested as the highest form of perfection and the highest perfection of form in art.

From the principle which we have formulated we cannot derive any detailed rules. Similarities and differences between extra-aesthetic values as well as their mastery by a perceiver, can be accomplished—taking the same material artifact—in an infinite number of ways. This is due to the infinite variety of possible clashes between a work and the development of artistic structure, and between the work and the development of society.

We were already aware of this fact when we posed the question of independently valid aesthetic values. But it was essential to attempt a solution of it, since only the hypothesis of an objective aesthetic value, constantly being perceived anew and realized anew in the most varied modifications, gives any meaning to the historical development of art. Only through this hypothesis can we explain the spirit of the constantly repeated attempts to create the perfect work of art, as well as the recurring of previously established values (e.g. the development of modern drama was governed by constantly renewed incursions of several enduring values such as the works of Shakespeare, Molière, etc.) It is thus necessary for any theory of aesthetic value to deal with the problem of objective, independent value, even when this theory treats the irreducible changeability of real-life evaluations of works of art. The import of the problem of independent aesthetic value is still more evident when we attempt to solve it, since we are led to the most fundamental task of art, which is the control and renewal of the ties between man and reality as an element of human behavior.

## IV

In the previous three chapters of this work we dealt with three interrelated concepts: aesthetic function, norm and value. We added the term "social facts," not only in order to qualify its relationship to the matter at hand, but also in an attempt to show that an abstract noetic analysis of the basis and scope of aesthetic function, norm and value must start from the social nature of the three phenomena. The position of either metaphysics or psychology with respect to aesthetics ought, by rights, to be occupied by sociology. The noetic investigation of the entire problem of aesthetic phenomena, being the proper task of aesthetics, must be based on the assumption that aesthetic function, norm and value are valid only in relation to man, and then only to man as a social product.

Aesthetic *function* is one of the most important agencies in human affairs. It can accompany every human act, and every object can manifest it. Aesthetic function is not a mere, practically unimportant, epiphenomenon of other functions, but is a co-determinant of human reaction to reality. Thus, for example, it is operative in the rearrangement of an object within the hierarchy of functions in that it attaches the object to a new dominant function, strengthening that function, calling attention to it, and elevating it above the others. Or again it supplants a lost function of an object or institution which has lost a temporary function and preserves it for new use and new functions, etc. In this way the aesthetic function is anchored in social behavior.

The aesthetic *norm,* the regulator of the aesthetic function, is not an unchanging law, but a process which is constantly being renewed. By its distribution in strata of older and newer norms, lower and higher, etc., and by its evolutionary transformations, it is incorporated into social evolution, sometimes indicating exclusive membership in a given social milieu, sometimes individual shifts from stratum to stratum, or, finally, accompanying and signalling shifts in the total structure of society.

Lastly, aesthetic value, which has special importance in art, where the aesthetic norm is more violated than observed, is basically a social phenomenon. Not only the changeability of real-life aesthetic evaluation but also stability of objective aesthetic value must be derived from contact between art and society. Aesthetic value enters into a close relationship with the extra-aesthetic values which a work contains, and, through their agency, with the system of values which determine the life practice of that collective which perceives the work. The relationship of aesthetic value to extra-aesthetic values is such that it dominates over the others, but does not disturb them, only joining them into a whole. Each value, of course, is removed from direct contact with a similar value which has practical validity. On the other hand, the relationship makes possible an active connection of the entire assembly of extra-aesthetic values in a work to the total attitude to reality taken by individuals as members of a collective for the sake of action. Through aesthetic value art also directly affects the emotional and volitional relation of man to the world, interfering with the regulator of human activity and thought (as distinct from science and philosophy which influence human activity through the thought process).

Thus the aesthetic realm, i.e. the realm of aesthetic function, norm and value, is broadly distributed over the entire area of human affairs, and is an important and many-sided agent of life practice. Those aesthetic theories which limit this realm to a few of its many aspects, which proclaim only pleasure or sensual excitement or expression or cognition, etc., do not do justice to its scope and importance. All these aspects, and many others, are embraced by the aesthetic, particularly in its highest manifestation, art. But to each of them belongs only that role which they exercise in shaping the total attitude of man to the world.

Prague, 1936.

# AFTERWORD

Jan Mukařovský has stated that his views in the late 1920's and early 1930's were close to those of the Russian Formalists, and that he began to part from a Formalist approach to art in 1934.[1] He and the Formalists shared interests in concepts such as form and function, but Mukařovský eventually placed some of the Formalist concepts into a perspective which differed from the one they had employed.

Mukařovský begins *Aesthetic Function, Norm and Value as Social Facts* with a discussion of the aesthetic function. This function is different from all other functions which an object or event may possess or exhibit. If the aesthetic function dominates the other functions it isolates an event or object from their extra-aesthetic surroundings, focuses the perceiver's attention on them, and (at least potentially) gives pleasure to the perceiver. In effect, dominance of the aesthetic function is, for Mukařovský, synonymous with the definition of art. Note that we are dealing with a *function,* and therefore with an actual or potential social situation. Accordingly, Mukařovský stresses, the aesthetic function is not a permanent or inevitable property of an event or object, but is evoked only when it is called upon by society to serve in some capacity or other.

Mukařovský appears to recapitulate most of the thinking of the Russian Formalists Boris Èjxenbaum and

[1] Jan Mukařovský: *"Předmluva k prvnímu vyddní," Kapitoly z české poetiky,* 2nd e., Prague, 1948, Vol. I, p. 9.

Jurij Tynjanov in regard to the concept of *dominanta:* ". . . the 'preeminent component or group of components,' which insures the unity of the work of literature as well as its 'perceptibility,' i.e., the fact that it is recognized as a literary phenomenon. In other words, the 'dominant quality' of literature is also its distinguishing feature, the core of its 'literariness'."[2] His "aesthetic function" has much in common with the Russian Formalists' "dominant," and when the aesthetic function dominates, the result is a work of art. Mukařovský proceeded to look at implications involving the world outside of art, thus moving in a direction opposite to that taken by the early Formalists. There is ample evidence in Tynjanov's "Literary Evolution" that he too was moving in much the same direction.[3] The inclusion of social environment in an article by Éjxenbaum is a further indication that the final stage of Russian Formalism had also begun to take an interest in extra-aesthetic matters.[4]

The establishment of the presence of the aesthetic function is a *social* phenomenon, and it involves a public which somehow becomes aware of the aesthetic function and makes a decision that it is or is not present in an object or event, and further decides, if it is present, whether it is in a dominant or a subordinate role. An object or event in which the aesthetic function participates and dominates will have special properties. Artistic considerations become the most important ones. Other functions such as communication, eroticism, etc. become subordinated in the hierarchy of functions. Furthermore,

[2]Victor Erlich: *Russian Formalism,* 2nd ed., The Hague, 1965, p. 199.

[3]Jurij Tynjanov: "O literaturnoj èvoljucii," *Arxaisty i novatory,* Leningrad, 1929, pp. 30-47.

[4]Cf. Erlich: p. 125.

these other functions, since they are not dominant, do not possess the same degree of urgency or significance that they would have in other circumstances.

\* \* \* \* \*

Unlike the aesthetic function, which is a dynamic concept involving dominance and subordination, the aesthetic *norm,* Mukařovský says, is constantly striving for stability and universal validity. Once again, of course, we are not speaking of an autonomous force, but rather of a social point of view, since the awareness of a norm implies that society knows both what constitutes any given norm and whether such a norm has been realized in a work of art.

Viewing art as a self-referential message which conveys something about its own organization, Mukařovský notes that the perceiving public comes to anticipate certain structural or organizational qualities from art, and thus exerts a normative influence on art. But, Mukařovský argues, if our anticipations are too frequently catered to, art will become automatic, boring, a cliché.[5] Furthermore, every time a norm is applied it is in a different social (and artistic) context. Thus, on the one hand, artists do not remain content to produce a series of clichés, but rather they violate norms, however slightly, in order to provoke interest and, on the other hand, sequential application or anticipation of a particular norm occur in changing social situations. Hence the fate of the norm is to be constantly changed (violated).

The importance of the aesthetic norm is certainly not diminished simply because it is constantly in

[5]Cf. René Wellek and Austin Warren: *Theory of Literature,* New York, 1956, p. 232.

flux.[6] Both artists and the public would be totally unable to exercise value judgements about art if they did not have an awareness of aesthetic norms. Mukařovský makes the point that even "lofty" art inevitably violates some aspects of a norm while adhering to others.

Just as in the case of the aesthetic function, Mukařovský's treatment of the aesthetic norm is reminiscent of Formalist positions. Viktor Šklovskij invented a term, "ostranenie" (making strange), which, in effect, described violation of an anticipated aesthetic norm.[7]

Once again the response to a concept had different implications for the early Russian Formalists than it did for Mukařovský. Having established both the norm and its constant alteration, the Formalists were primarily interested in the effects of such alteration on literature (styles, genres, etc.).[8] Mukařovský did not, of course, ignore these effects, but his primary concern lay in another direction. He wished to make it clear that whatever the concrete literary facts resulting from changing norms may be, the process of change itself is basically a social and not a literary mechanism, since it requires a social body which either produces a new norm (artists) or recognizes and eventually accepts a new norm (perceivers).

\* \* \* \* \*

Just as the aesthetic function inevitably finds itself regulated by norms, so do these norms depend on value judgements for their (however temporary) validity, and

---

[6]Cf. Erlich: p. 280. For a more extreme reaction cf. René Wellek: *The Literary Theory and Aesthetics of the Prague School, Michigan Slavic Contributions,* No. 2, Ann Arbor, 1969.

[7]Cf. Erlich: p. 76 and pp. 176-178.

[8]Ibid., pp. 252-260.

just as dominance of the aesthetic function can be concretely implemented in numerous ways depending on the prevailing norms, so does the development and alteration of the aesthetic norm depend on changes in the totality of aesthetic *values* manifested within the society which perceives and reacts to the norm.

Because the aesthetic function is the dominant function in a work of art, aesthetic values, according to Mukařovský, are also the dominant values. Other values are always present, to be sure, but they are in a subordinate position.

* * * * *

Mukařovský was able to place literary development and social influence in a logical perspective. He acknowledged that society can and does exert influence on art, but added that art responds most successfully through use of the components of its own medium.[9] A valuable aspect of Mukařovský's investigations into the relationships which exist between art and society is the two-fold viewpoint which they permit one to take with respect to the power of art and its effects on those who perceive art. We have noted the transformation of extra-aesthetic values when they come under the domination of the aesthetic function. The result is dominant, aesthetic values which are perceived simultaneously with subordinate, extra-aesthetic values. Even further: not only do we as perceivers confront material (in art) which has been taken from the extra-aesthetic realm, but we do so under circumstances which are themselves extra-aesthetic. The totality of our confrontations with a work of art, or

---

[9]Jan Mukařovský *et al: Torso a tajemství Máchova díla*, Prague, 1938, p. 9.

with art in general, also influences our perceptions. The interrelation of art and society is actually even more complex, since both of the above-mentioned confrontations between aesthetic and extra-aesthetic considerations occur simultaneously: a) a perceiver deals with aesthetic material while in a non-aesthetic situation and b) the material being perceived presents to him both its extra-aesthetic, material ties with the world of experience and its aesthetically valid and relevant aspects. These considerations indicate the consistency of the systematic approach of the Prague School, and we concur with Professor Wellek that Mukařovský "kept an admirable balance between close observation and bold speculation and propounded a literary theory which illuminates the structure of the work of art, its relation to . . . the history of literature, both as literature and social fact.[10]

Mark E. Suino

[10]René Wellek: *The Literary Theory and Aesthetics of the Prague School, Michigan Slavic Contributions*, No. 2, p. 33.